ADVANCE PRAISE

"An engaging story that teaches brilliant lessons on true prosperity. Leisa Peterson guides you toward the abundance you deserve and can surely attain."
—Bob Burg, Coauthor of *The Go-Giver*

"In this must-read book, Leisa Peterson delivers essential money wisdom with clarity, heart, and transformative insight."
—Barbara Huson, Author of *Overcoming Underearning* and *Rewire for Wealth*

"This is deeply effective on a level that I haven't read before. By the end of the first chapter I was already considering my own money values in a way that I have never truly reflected on before."
—David Ralph, Host of the Join Up Dots podcast

"This transformative parable goes beyond wealth accumulation, offering a powerful roadmap to aligning your financial decisions with your deepest values."
—Jordan Grumet, Author of *Taking Stock and The Purpose Code* and host of the Earn & Invest Podcast.

"If you've ever felt stuck in worry about money or sensed there must be a better way to approach your finances, this book will feel like a warm hug and a gentle push in a wonderful new direction!"
—Marilyn Alauria, Author, Purpose to profit coach

"I didn't expect a money book to move me this much. Leisa's story-driven approach is powerful, relatable, and very inspiring."
—Michelle Schroeder-Gardner, Making Sense of Cents

"Mirabel asks the important and difficult questions when shifting past beliefs about money to a new reality of holding more abundance. We can all relate to her journey of self-discovery and celebrate the unfurling of her awareness that abundance is infinite."
—Lisa Fraley, Attorney and author of *Easy Legal Steps That Are Also Good For Your Soul*

"One of the hardest things for any of us is feeling alone and unseen. Through this book, in the example of Mirabel, I suspect there are many

women who will see themselves. That's where the catalysis begins."
—Danny Iny, Founder/CEO at Mirasee

"Through the compelling and relatable story of Mirabel paired with insightful self-reflection journaling prompts, I found myself rethinking my own beliefs about money in a profound way."
—Elizabeth Sinclair, Strategist

"What I love most about this book is how it seamlessly blends personal growth with financial empowerment, reminding us that true prosperity starts from within."
—Jayne Warrilow, Founder of Sacred Changemakers and best-selling author of *Beyond Profit*

"Leisa Peterson has a way of making you stop, reflect, and completely rethink your relationship with wealth. It's insightful, inspiring, and packed with those 'aha!' moments that stick with you long after you turn the last page."
—Dan Haylett, Financial Planner and Host of Humans vs Retirement podcast

"The Money Catalyst is a beautiful book that grabbed me from the first paragraph and gave me a framework to approach these changes more intentionally."
—Gerri Detweiler, Financial author, speaker and writer

"This book is the perfect guide on how to define what abundance means to you, build wealth with meaning, and learn how to be present to the joy of life."
—Jessica Moorhouse, Bestselling author of *Everything but Money* and host of the More Money Podcast

"Through the story of Mirabel, practical exercises and insightful reflections, Leisa's book helps you unlock your financial potential and create a life of abundance and freedom."
—Steven Morris, Business strategist and coach, author of *The Beautiful Business*

"Leisa Peterson helps you break free from limiting money habits and step into a life of abundance, clarity, and possibility."
—Joe Saul-Sehy, Creator, Co-host Stacking Benjamins podcast

"Her ability to articulate the emotional and psychological aspects of money is remarkable. The book doesn't just offer tools; it offers understanding."
—Sarah Santacroce, Humane marketing advocate and author of *Selling Like We're Human* and *Marketing Like We're Human*

"The Money Catalyst teaches us how to shift our perspective on money so that we are open to the joys, opportunities, and connections that flow into our lives."
—David Stein, Money for the Rest of Us

"Thanks to her intoxicating writing, that journey is both easy, interesting and revelational."
—Tom Poland, Chief Leadsologist, Leadsology

"I highly recommend reading The Money Catalyst if you want to make real changes in how you approach life, and find more ease and joy!"
—Patty Block, The Block Group

"The Money Catalyst masterfully unpacks the complexities of achieving financial abundance and freedom—not by offering detailed money management strategies, but by helping readers break through the deep-seated unconscious blocks."
—Lisa Merlo-Booth, Paradigm-shifting relationship coach

"As a husband, this book helped me understand my wife's perspective on money and relationships with greater clarity. And as an individual, it revealed where I can grow in abundance and financial harmony."
—Ed Coambs, Founder of HealthyLoveandMoney.com

"Leisa Peterson does it again; bringing new perspectives and awakenings around prosperity, money, and fulfillment in this delightful novel. Let The Money Catalyst be a reminder of grounding true wealth, beginning from the inside out."

—SIMRAN, Author, creator of the 11:11 Magazine and 11:11 Talk Radio Steward

THE MONEY CATALYST

A STORY ABOUT DISCOVERING ABUNDANCE

LEISA PETERSON

WEALTHCLINIC, LLC

Contents

A New Way of Seeing

Jenny cradled the éclair like a precious jewel, her eyes wide with wonder. "It's exquisite," she whispered, studying it from every angle before inhaling its rich aroma.

Outside our tiny Parisian café, rain drummed against centuries-old cobblestones. We'd ducked in here to escape the downpour. Now, I wrapped my chilled fingers around a cup of chocolat chaud—thick, velvety hot chocolate that poured like liquid silk. Steam rose in delicate wisps as I watched my friend fall in love with a pastry.

"Isn't it the most magnificent éclair you've ever seen?" she asked, tears of joy welling in her eyes.

"Yes!" I found myself crying too, not entirely sure why.

Sunlight pierced the clouds, streaming through the café windows and casting long shadows across our table. I realized I was witnessing something extraordinary: a woman embodying the art of living, teaching me a masterclass in presence.

I had invited Jenny to Paris for ten days to thank her for inspiring my first book, *The Mindful Millionaire*. For three decades, I'd taught others how to build wealth, written about it, and lived it. I thought

I understood what mattered most about money. Those ten days with Jenny changed everything.

While other tourists rushed to squeeze in all the famous sites, Jenny found magic everywhere. Her face would light up mid-stride. "Look at those rose bushes!" she'd exclaim, stopping to marvel at their graceful archways over ancient stone walls. She wasn't saving her joy for a milestone moment—she lived fully in the now.

On my flight back home, I watched a movie about a man who waited for a terminal diagnosis to start really living. But Jenny had already taught me better. She'd shown me how fear holds us back and it takes courage to claim our lives right now. In Paris, I saw what happens when we settle for less than our dreams. Seeing the man in the movie realize he'd lost his one chance with life broke me wide open. The comfortable lies I'd been telling myself about 'someday' and 'when the time is right' crumbled away. This truth grew into the book you now hold: *The Money Catalyst.*

Perhaps you know that persistent whisper of "not enough"? That nagging sense that something essential is missing, regardless of your financial situation? We all tell ourselves stories about when we will finally feel satisfied—after we get the next promotion, when we pay off debts, or once we save enough. These familiar "someday" stories become the invisible walls of our own making.

But there are other stories—stories that set us free. Throughout history, storytelling has been humanity's most profound teacher. When facts and figures fade from memory, stories endure. They slip past our mental defenses and plant seeds of wisdom directly in our hearts, taking root in ways that mere instruction never could.

You're about to embark on such a story—one that might just transform your own. Meet Mirabel, who on paper has it all: the career, the relationship, the lifestyle. Yet like many of us, she senses a deeper calling, a whisper of possibility that won't let her rest. Her journey mirrors questions you might ask: What am I really meant to do? Is there more to my life than what I thought I was supposed to do? Can the life I imagine in my dreams become real?

Enter the Money Catalyst, your guide to illuminating hidden pathways and possibilities. Like its chemical namesake, it accelerates transformation via eight powerful Catalysts. Through Mirabel's journey, you'll discover how to break free from old patterns, uncover what truly matters to you, and build a life of deep meaning.

As you experience Mirabel's story, you'll discover what becomes possible when you refuse to accept limits. You'll face moments that challenge your deepest beliefs about money and success, pushing you into uncomfortable territory. After you've traveled with her through her complete transformation, you'll find guided journaling questions waiting for you—an invitation to revisit her journey while exploring your own. It's in these very moments of reflection that the most powerful breakthroughs emerge, and your own story of expansion begins to unfold.

This is the guide I wish someone had given me many years ago—a roadmap for creating a life of genuine fulfillment. In today's increasingly complex world, finding your path and building wealth can feel overwhelming. These pages will light your way forward, helping you avoid the costly detours that keep so many stuck, so you can live more and stress less. Be sure to take advantage of your special gifts including a 47 page companion journal ($10 value) by registering your purchase at www.moneycatalystbook.com.

Are you ready to begin? Take a deep breath and turn the page. Your journey through the eight catalysts awaits—and I promise, it will change everything.

Catalyst One

Awaken to Possibility

"We delight in the beauty of the butterfly, but rarely admit the changes it has gone through to achieve that beauty."
~Maya Angelou

Mirabel watched Leila glide down the busy San Francisco street, long red hair blowing in the wind. Her colorful sundress flowed around her as she moved to a beat only she could hear. Mirabel knew Leila didn't care what others thought was "normal." She only wanted to live life to the fullest.

Passing gray buildings on her way to their favorite lunch spot, Leila stood out like a rainbow in a black-and-white world. She was happy, unlike many around her. Perhaps her unique upbringing explained it.

Leila had shared with Mirabel that her mom had been a free spirit. They had lived in a van, roaming from town to town for various jobs. Despite their lack of material wealth, those years had been rich with outdoor adventures and freedom. Mirabel often thought back to this conversation from several months ago, when she and Leila first became friends at work.

"That nomadic lifestyle taught me that good things can happen, even in tough times," she'd said. She developed an eye for life's free wonders, like city lights, butterflies in parks, and golden sunsets over the ocean. "Little things, little moments of beauty fill me with awe and gratitude."

Mirabel knew Leila could find joy in any situation.

When Leila was 19, her mother's passing left her navigating the world alone. She couch-surfed between friends' homes, working a string of menial jobs to survive. Her bosses exploited her vulnerability, knowing she couldn't afford to quit. Friends' sympathy gradually wore thin, and dinner often meant ramen. She faced the unique exhaustion of being young and untethered, carrying both her mother's free spirit and the weight of her absence.

Yet beneath the daily struggle, Leila gradually built something that wasn't quite optimism, but a hard-earned kind of wisdom. "Challenges help me grow," she'd say during her better moments, her voice quiet but steady. The words weren't a shield against pain or a denial of darkness—they were a truth she'd fought for, lost, and found again countless times. Some days, the weight felt crushing. Other days, she could trace how each setback had forced her to discover strengths she never knew she had.

She told Mirabel that in her lowest moments, she'd sit in public parks. She ached for her mother and wondered if resilience was just a word for having no choice. But, season by season, she began to see things differently. Her will to find meaning in the struggle was more than survival. It was a messy, imperfect triumph.

By her mid-30s, Leila had built a successful career as a web developer. Her grace and kindness put everyone at ease, qualities that drew Mirabel to her immediately. Despite—or perhaps because of—her unusual upbringing, Leila moved through life with a buoyancy that made her stand out. What began as casual workplace conversations between Mirabel and Leila quickly deepened into a friendship built on shared understanding.

Though both had known poverty's sting, Mirabel and Leila's childhoods painted vastly different portraits. Leila's life had been rich in starry skies and open roads, her mother turning the van they lived in into an endless adventure. Mirabel's world, by contrast, had been confined to a cramped apartment, where her mother's endless work hours barely kept them afloat, and "We can't afford that" became a familiar refrain.

What struck both women was how their similar backgrounds had shaped such different outlooks. Leila had learned to embrace what life offered, finding joy in small moments, while Mirabel lived in constant worry that there would never be enough. Growing up with so little had taught them both to get by, yet Leila saw open doors where Mirabel saw walls.

Even with a well-paying job as a marketing manager, Mirabel couldn't escape her childhood fears. Her life with Ethan, her cautious planner of a husband, brought financial stability, yet every optional expense sparked familiar anxieties. She'd freeze at checkout screens, second-guess restaurant choices, and spiral into worst-case scenarios. Even suggesting donations to meaningful causes like her friend Tanya's nonprofit sparked tension, with Ethan's scrutiny of each unbudgeted dollar reinforcing her belief that any "extra" was a dangerous indulgence.

While Leila saw each new day as a fresh canvas of possibilities, Mirabel scanned for storms. "When you've lived with so little for so long," Leila would say, "you learn to appreciate what's available right now." But for Mirabel, each achievement only heightened her fear of loss. At work, this manifested in her meticulous approach to projects, her serious demeanor a stark contrast to Leila's natural cheerfulness. Yet something in her friend's carefree grace called to her, like a half-remembered song from childhood.

Their weekly lunch dates had become Mirabel's favorite escape from work pressures. Today, as they settled into their usual corner table, Leila could barely contain her excitement.

"I know we talked about going on a trip when we're done with the big project at work," she said.

"We are so close!" Mirabel added, excitedly. They'd been working on this project for months and there was a bonus attached to completion.

"We are!" Leila said. "What would you say to celebrating the end of this project phase with a trip to Paris?"

Mirabel felt her shoulders tighten. "I don't know, Leila. It's a big expense and I'm not sure I can afford it right now." The words tumbled out automatically—her practiced shield against any threat to her careful life. She'd perfected this response over the years, using money worries like a sword to cut down every chance at adventure before it could take root.

Leila leaned in with a gentle smile. "Remember our conversation a few weeks ago? Your sister's new airline job means almost-free flights, right? I've found some charming B'n'Bs that won't break the bank. With the travel savings, Paris is actually doable. We've worked so hard—don't you think we deserve a little adventure?"

Mirabel felt the pull of possibility. She caught herself reaching for her phone to check her bank balance, then remembered her sister Sarah mentioning midweek availability on the SFO-Paris route. With Ethan traveling for his project right after her work deadline...

"You know what, Leila?" Mirabel's face lit up with a sudden decision. "Let's do it! Paris, here we come!"

From their first morning in Paris, the contrast in their mindsets was clear. Mirabel fretted over every euro. Leila soaked up the Parisian vibe like a wildflower in sunlight.

The pattern started at the airport. Mirabel wanted to take the train into Paris, but Leila convinced her to split a rideshare instead. It cost fifteen euros more each, but they wouldn't have to drag their bags through the metro. Stepping out of the car as they arrived at their B'n'B, Mirabel felt the usual guilt about spending the extra money.

After lugging their bags up five flights of worn wooden stairs, Mirabel collapsed onto the sofa. Rays of sunlight streamed through the narrow window, casting long shadows on the uneven floorboards. Despite its tiny size and budget price, the apartment was cozy. Something about it made her breath catch. Though, maybe it was just the stairs.

"You know," Mirabel said, still winded, "Ethan wasn't thrilled about me spending money on this trip. Made me promise to watch every euro while I'm here." She sighed. "But he knew how much I needed this break. The timing worked out perfectly—him being at that client installation while I'm in Paris. I'm sure a little time apart will be healthy for us."

Mirabel watched as Leila crossed to the window, pushing it open. Her friend's silhouette stirred her with emotion. She'd seen pictures of Paris, of course. But, nothing had prepared her for this: the afternoon light on the ancient chimneys and shiny rooftops. The city seemed to stretch endlessly toward the horizon.

Leaning out the window, Leila breathed in the air with childlike wonder. "I can't believe we're actually here," she exclaimed. Her raw joy made Mirabel's usual anxieties feel paper-thin and distant.

As they unpacked, Mirabel folded a sweater, still amazed at their spontaneity. "I can't believe how quickly we pulled this off! When I asked Aisha for time off, she just said 'Of course, you've earned it!' and offered to cover my team."

"Such a different world from my first real job," Leila said as she arranged her toiletries. "My old boss used to make us beg for every single day off, like we were asking for the moon."

"I'm just grateful to finally have a boss who wants me to grow and enjoy life," Mirabel replied.

"And speaking of enjoying life," Leila said. "Paris is waiting."

To fight the jet lag, they grabbed warm falafel and let the city guide them through its narrow streets. Window boxes overflowed with red geraniums. Cafés spilled onto the sidewalks. Each corner revealed a post-card-perfect scene. Mirabel's money worries began fading like morning mist. This was Paris, after all. When had she last felt so light?

As evening approached, Leila pulled up a chic restaurant's menu on her phone. "This place gets amazing reviews. And I can't believe it, but they have a lunch spot open tomorrow!" Mirabel's first instinct was to calculate costs, but something had shifted. Looking at her friend's bright, expectant face, she felt her usual caution melt away. "You know what? Let's go all-out for our first real French meal!"

The next day, they were led through a vine-covered courtyard to their table. As they studied the menu, Mirabel took in the scene—elegantly dressed patrons, birds flitting between vines, the soft murmur of the stone fountain. Leila's infectious excitement overwhelmed her usual caution—silencing even Ethan's voice in her head warning about expenses. "Should we split a bottle of wine?" she asked before she could second-guess herself. Leila's eyes sparkled. "Let's make it champagne!"

They watched the golden bubbles fizz as the wine steward poured. Leila raised her glass with a smile. "To embracing every bit of life's magic!"

Over the next few hours, Mirabel and Leila enjoyed the nine-course tasting menu. They savored each part, letting their senses experience each dish. The foie gras melted on their tongues. The black truffle cheese released an earthy smell. The bright Normandy butter lingered with the tender sea scallops.

The mid-afternoon sun warmed Mirabel's shoulders as she settled deeper into her chair, feeling happier than she had in months. The champagne and the magic of Paris eased her self-consciousness. Their conversation flowed and she was completely present. They paused, now and then, to savor another exquisite bite. Their laughter mixed with the gentle clink of glasses as they toasted to the "City of Lights" and their glowing friendship.

Mirabel's heart lifted at the sight of the waiter approaching with his cart, wielding a small torch with ceremony. She held her breath as he lowered the flame to their crème brûlées, watching the sugar crystals melt into a glossy amber sheet. When the espresso arrived, its rich aroma embraced her. It mingled with the scent of caramelized sugar and warm vanilla. She caught Leila's eye across the table and saw her own delight mirrored there.

"Sometimes the smallest moments are the sweetest," Leila said. "Like right now—good food, great company, watching the world go by. This is what I live for."

Mirabel smiled, feeling totally caught up in the moment. "This is the best lunch I've ever had. And not just because of the food."

"Well," Leila grinned, "we're just getting started. Paris has so much more to show us."

That first lunch cast its spell. Mirabel wandered the streets with fresh eyes, drinking in the melody of street musicians, the warmth of fresh bread, and the buttery perfume of morning croissants.

Even simple activities like sipping coffee at a sidewalk café took on a romantic air. Mirabel felt like she was starring in her own French movie adventure. The bright blue sky and historic buildings were a breathtaking backdrop.

One crisp morning, as they strolled along the Seine River, Leila breathed in the lively atmosphere and suggested a privately guided tour at the Louvre Museum. Mirabel felt the usual pang of apprehension over the cost but eventually agreed.

As the tour proceeded through the hallowed halls, Mirabel found herself completely transfixed. François, their quirky art historian guide, brought every painting and sculpture to life with his vivid stories and insights. Mirabel hung on his every word as he transformed dry facts from plaques into gripping human dramas.

At the Mona Lisa, while the usual crowd jostled for photos, François guided them to an overlooked spot. "There she is," he sighed. "Do you know why her smile is so enigmatic? Legends say da Vinci employed court jesters who performed outrageous acts while she posed. Her barely perceptible smile is the hint of amusement she could not suppress!"

Leila's eyes widened in delight, but Mirabel was utterly transported. She no longer saw just an ordinary portrait but glimpsed the daily life of a Renaissance-era beauty, her likeness being captured by the whims of a creative genius. From that moment on, Mirabel saw the entire museum with new eyes. The tour had unlocked a world she'd never experienced before, her fear of missing out transforming into a drive to miss nothing.

Before leaving the Louvre, they wandered into the museum store, where a leather-bound journal caught Mirabel's eye. The embossed cover with intricate patterns reminded her of the architectural details they'd seen that day. She ran her fingers over the textured surface, surprised by her attraction to it. She'd never been one to keep a journal—had always thought it self-indulgent somehow. But now, standing amid the echoes of centuries of art and human expression, she felt drawn to its blank pages. They promised a space to capture her shifting views of herself and the world. Without overthinking it, she bought the journal, tucking it into her bag like a secret promise to herself.

In their remaining days in Paris, Leila's enthusiasm guided their adventures. Mirabel found herself instinctively mirroring her friend's joy of living and felt like something had shifted. She no longer fixated on the "extras" or counted costs. Instead, she was finally free to savor the richness of every experience.

One big moment came when Mirabel asked Leila why she was tipping a talented street artist so much. She warned, "I don't get it, isn't that a lot of money for something you can't even take with you?!"

Leila challenged Mirabel's view. She said, "If we follow that logic, this trip is a waste of money. The memories won't last forever. But isn't experiencing beauty and feeling alive what truly makes us feel wealthy? That's what living an abundant life is all about."

Mirabel was struck by a sudden realization. For as long as she could remember she and Ethan had been focused exclusively on stockpiling their savings. They were depriving themselves of joy for the sake of security. Now, she understood how Leila's mindset helped her feel so good and how much she enjoyed sharing her joy with others.

On the final evening of their trip, they visited Le Tout-Paris, one of the city's best rooftop bars. They sipped exotic mocktails and watched the pink and blue sunset colors washing over the iconic skyline. Mirabel edged closer to Leila.

Her throat felt tight. "This trip has been amazing. It's shown me how afraid I've been," she whispered, "of never having enough. Of losing what I have. And watching you these past few days..." She trailed off, searching for words that felt too big to name.

Leila just listened; present in that way she had always been.

"You just... dive in. Into moments. Into joy." Mirabel's voice cracked slightly. "While I've been standing at the edge, counting my steps, measuring everything." She finally looked up at her friend, eyes bright. "I'm so tired of living like that."

Leila reached across the table and laid her hand against Mirabel's wrist. "When we spend on what nourishes the soul, our life becomes rich."

Mirabel let out a shaky breath. Something was changing inside her—not a clean breakthrough, but a crack in old foundations. She didn't have the words for it yet. But sitting here, under the Parisian sky, she felt the first taste of what it might mean to live differently. To finally claim her place in her own life, not as an apology, but as a right.

As the last light faded from the sky, they tipped their glasses again and savored the final hours of their trip together.

Mirabel strolled her suitcase through the busy departure terminal at Charles de Gaulle Airport. She and Leila had bid their farewells earlier, their paths separating for different flights back to San Francisco.

A tinge of sadness had crept in. The transformative Paris trip was ending. But, it left her with a renewed sense of determination. No longer would she allow her growth to be held back by her fears. This vacation had expanded her mindset—all that remained was to lean into what she'd learned.

Approaching her gate, she saw the monitor: a four-hour delay for her standby flight. Her initial grimace at the thought of overpriced airport food faded as she remembered her credit card's lounge access. Her steps quickened, eager for a quiet space to reflect on her transformative week in Paris.

In a peaceful corner of the lounge, she sank into a plush chair. Gourmet pastries, craft coffee, reliable Wi-Fi—all included. This unexpected pause felt like a gift, one last moment to savor before returning to life back home.

Mirabel pulled out her phone, smiling as she typed a message to Ethan: *Can't wait to be home with you. I miss you so much.* Then to Sarah: *Thanks again for the airline perks, sis. Paris was incredible! Can't wait to tell you all about it.*

As she scrolled through her photos, lost in her Parisian memories, a voice cut through her reverie.

"Is this seat open?" she looked up to find an older gentleman gesturing to the chair beside her. His unconventional style caught her eye immediately—a bright linen shirt paired with terracotta pants and striking turquoise loafers. "Yes, it is," she replied.

Once he was situated, he turned and asked where her travels were taking her in a friendly voice.

"San Francisco," she answered.

"The Bay Area, how wonderful!" the man exclaimed in a Southern drawl. "I'm headed home to South Carolina."

As they exchanged small talk about their trips, Mirabel noted how open the stranger's energy was, his warmth unrestrained and welcoming.

She couldn't help but study how he carried himself with an almost whimsical air, his Bohemian clothes offset by subtle hints of wealth—a gold watch bearing the iconic Cartier insignia, a leather tote bag that was distinctly Hermès, and beaded bracelets studded with what appeared to be precious gemstones.

His grooming spoke of the same careful attention to uniqueness: closely cropped, salt-and-pepper hair shaved in an intricate pattern, complemented by a neat goatee and mustache that framed his animated mouth. Though Mirabel guessed he was in his early 60s, his eyes sparkled with a lively energy that seemed ageless.

"Paris shifted something in me," she found herself saying, surprised by her candor.

"Paris has a way of doing that to all of us," he chuckled with an air of knowing. "I'm curious to hear more about what happened for you. That is, if you're okay with sharing."

Mirabel felt herself relaxing in the stranger's presence. She felt no superficial pretense about him, only a genuine zest for life.

She recounted some standout moments from her Paris awakening, including the extravagant nine-course tasting menu she'd surprised herself by indulging in. The man listened with rapt attention, his eyes lighting up.

"Wow!" he exclaimed. "Yes, the art of savoring! How wonderful—it sounds like a masterclass in being present to the joyfulness of life."

She shared how her friend Leila had role-modeled an energy filled with gratitude.

He nodded. "What a gift, to have such a dazzling guide! We'd all do well to evoke more childlike wonder in our daily lives."

Mirabel enjoyed the man's genuine interest.

"You know," she continued, "I had an amazing time in Paris. But, I learned something about myself there that I'm not proud of."

"And what was that?" He replied with eyebrows raised.

She took a deep breath before she spoke. "I've come to see that I haven't been living fully. I earn a good income, but I'm always worrying about money. As a result, I've missed many of the joys and opportunities life offers. I've been too caught up in money fears to truly enjoy the moment."

"I understand," the stranger said with a thoughtful nod. "I used to be trapped in that same mindset you're describing. It took me years to even realize I had a problem—I only knew how to work hard and harder. I grew my company from a startup to $5 million in revenue, then $10 million, $50 million... But no matter how well we did, I kept pushing myself." He shook his head. "I was single for a long time because work was my entire life. Even after I fell in love and started a family... They suffered from my absence and obsession with the business."

Mirabel leaned in.

His expression grew somber. "But that wasn't all. The problem went deeper—I didn't know how to have fun. How to relax. How to enjoy the moment. There was so much about living that I'd never been taught." He let out a chuckle. "My friends definitely thought I was a total bore back then. I'd pass on any chances to travel or socialize. I'd see them as frivolous alcohol-inspired write-offs. I turned up my nose at anything spiritual or 'New Age,' even though a part of me was always intrigued by those ideas."

Mirabel was transfixed by the stranger's honesty.

He gave a heavy sigh, then continued, "The truth is, I turned off any glimmer of inner light or joy within me. Sacrificed it all in the never-ending pursuit of money and status. All that mattered was growing that company bigger, no matter what it cost me."

"I can relate to so much of what you're saying," Mirabel said when he finished. "This driven, workaholic approach robs us."

The man nodded. "Indeed, it does. For far too long, I let fears and limiting beliefs dictate how I operated in this world. Always striving, never arriving. I was always chasing some unclear idea of success. But, I never let myself feel successful." He leaned back, taking a sip of his coffee. "My awakening began when I was diagnosed with cancer. Staring your own mortality in the face—it shakes you to your core. Forces you to re-evaluate what matters."

"Oh, wow," she said.

"Thankfully I now see cancer as a gift. It woke me up to what life is about. Going through treatment slowed me down and forced me to take stock. The good news is that I beat it—or that's what the doctors say. Looking back, I could swear that my higher self knew this would get my attention. And it worked!"

Mirabel felt her eyes welling up as she related to much of what he shared. "I'm glad you're better and can see cancer as a gift. That's pretty incredible. I'm grateful I've had this experience in Paris. Maybe it will help me to re-evaluate my choices. I'm sorry it took getting cancer to do that for you."

"It is what it is," the man replied. "The key is being open to the lessons as they appear, no matter how difficult or uncomfortable. I'll admit, at first, I resisted fiercely against making any real changes."

She nodded, feeling a surge of empathy. "It's incredible how life can nudge us toward growth, even in the midst of our resistance."

He chuckled. "I understand embracing nudges. In fact, after my cancer diagnosis, I hired a coach. Can you imagine, a self-professed personal growth skeptic hiring a life coach? My family thought I'd lost my marbles after the cancer treatments. But I knew deep down I needed outside support to uproot such ingrained patterns."

She felt a sense of courage blossoming inside herself.

"So, this life coach... What kind of tools or practices did they have you implement?" She was hungry to learn more.

The man smiled. "The first big mindset shift she had me work on was to replace guilt and shame with self-compassion. For decades, I'd mentally beaten myself up. I did it anytime I deviated from my harsh, perfectionist mindset. She taught me to approach myself with more gentleness."

"I love that. It's like my friend Leila was telling me—we have to give ourselves grace and stop being so punishing."

"That's a wonderful way to see it!" The man's eyes danced with enthusiasm. "Once I opened up some space for self-appreciation and acceptance, joy started flowing in. Small things brought me bliss—a cool breeze on a hot day, sunlight shimmering through trees, my children's laughter."

She found herself taking a deep breath, resonating with his words.

"But the real breakthrough," he continued, "came when she shared some simple but powerful advice. It's like she could see right through me...and said, "Don't always worry about what you lack. Focus on valuing what you have. Look for the hidden opportunities in every situation. Take responsibility for all parts of your life—the good and the bad."

"It was like being in a dark room. I was so focused on finding the light switch that I didn't notice the sunshine pouring through the window."

She nodded.

"Her advice opened the curtains," he continued. "I discovered that the room was flooded with light. I'd been surrounded by brightness all along. I just couldn't see it until I was ready." He shook his head. "From that day on, my whole approach to life shifted. I saw how there's a big difference between fulfillment and achieving goals. One is very rewarding but the other can ruin your life if you get too obsessed with it."

He leaned forward. "Abundant living is about fulfillment. It means feeling satisfied with yourself and your life. It's about focusing on what matters far more than what doesn't."

The man smiled and continued. "It's like there were two paths in front of me. One path was all about checking boxes. You had to get good grades, have an impressive company, and make a lot of money. But no matter how many proverbial boxes I checked, I never felt content or like I had enough."

"The other path was about cultivating an inner calm and peacefulness. It was about appreciating the journey itself, not just the destinations. That's the path of joy. It's about expressing thanks and finding enjoyment in simple things each day."

"Can you see the difference? Achievement is an endless ladder you'll never reach the top of. But fulfillment is being conscious and alive in this moment. It lacks nothing."

The man let out a contented sigh. "Once I got off that achievement ladder, I started to prioritize my fulfillment. Everything changed. I felt prosperous in ways money can't buy. My relationships improved. My health got better. Opportunities started flowing to me. I could finally see how it's an inside job!" He tilted his head, studying her expression and paused. "I know that's a lot to share but you inspired me. I'm curious what's coming up for you as you hear this?"

"Whoa, that's... incredible!" she said finally, shifting in her seat. "It sounds like working with your coach helped you let go of all that striving and stress? Changed your whole life? I think this is similar to what Leila was trying to show me in Paris."

"Yes," he replied. "And you're fortunate to have Leila as a friend. Most people miss figuring this out their entire lives."

Mirabel squinched up her eyes. "I'll be honest though... The idea of feeling abundant all the time and letting go of control feels very strange to me. I default to thinking logically. I need solid facts before I'll believe something. Anything too spiritual or mystical just makes me roll my eyes."

"Tell me more about that," he encouraged gently.

"In Paris, I kept getting pulled back into that negative cycle of guilt and fear. For brief moments, I'd feel that wonderful sense of freedom, like during that amazing lunch." Her eyes lit up remembering it. "But then, the critical voice in my head would say, 'You can't afford this. You're being reckless and irresponsible.' That voice is all I've ever known. The weird part is, I thought that voice was helping me!"

Mirabel's face clouded over as she realized this wasn't about the money. It was about how she was living. "As lovely as those free, amazing moments felt, they were flashes. My wiring feels locked in at this point. I'm not sure I can shift out of it, as much as I want to." She looked at the man with a pained expression. "Part of me is scared. If I let go of that controlling, critical voice, everything will fall apart."

The man nodded. "I know those fears well. Confronting our deepest beliefs can feel shaky and scary at first. But what you experienced in Paris is a start. You can do this."

He leaned back. "Our minds are logical and rational. They crave predictability, control, and hard data in order to make us feel safe. Embracing a prosperous mindset means being willing to face uncertainty. It's about loosening that death grip of control and allowing life to unfold."

Mirabel's eyes widened.

The man gave her a knowing look. "I know we've only just met, but I can see the idea both terrifies you and intrigues you. That critical voice will fight this transformation every step of the way. But I'm telling you—it's worth it."

She felt her chest tightening with longing and trepidation. She couldn't deny the part of her that craved a sense of freedom. But could she actually create it?

He fixed Mirabel with an intent gaze. "So, let me ask—now that your eyes are open, what's next? What are you dreaming of? How will you integrate an abundance mindset when you return home?"

She felt the immediate tug of her past habits getting in the way of trying something different. She also realized this change was hers alone to make.

Drawing a deep breath, she met his gaze. "I don't know. I don't understand what abundant living really means to me. But I know this week awakened me to greater possibilities. Something shifted, even if the path isn't clear."

She nodded to herself. "I can't go back to living the way I was. I want to embody this mindset."

Just then, the timer on her phone buzzed reminding her to head towards her gate. She stood and gathered her bags, turning back to the stranger.

"I'm Mirabel, by the way. What's your name?"

The man smiled. "Nice to meet you, Mirabel. I'm Lawrence."

Without pausing she blurted out. "I'm grateful for all you've shared. Would you mind if we kept in touch? I'd love to share how my journey unfolds."

"I'd be delighted to," Lawrence said, handing her his card. "Reach out anytime. And remember—a full life needs freedom. The path is different for each of us."

She took the card and tucked it safely into her backpack, feeling an undeniable spark of excitement at the prospect of staying in touch with Lawrence. His wisdom and guidance had already made an impact.

"Thank you, Lawrence," her voice filled with gratitude. "I can't tell you how much this means to me. Talking with you has given me a new sense of direction."

He nodded, his eyes twinkling. "Sometimes, all we need is a new perspective and encouragement to find our way. I have a feeling you're going to do great things, Mirabel. Just remember to stay true to yourself and trust in the journey."

Arriving at the gate, Mirabel stood near the boarding area, hoping for any available seat as a standby passenger. She couldn't believe her luck when tapped on her shoulder by an airline representative with a warm smile holding out a boarding pass. "We have a first-class seat available. You're all set."

She blinked, momentarily stunned. She'd never flown first class!

Settling into the luxurious leather seat, Mirabel nestled among the pillows and blankets, grateful for the perfect space to reflect into the week's unexpected turns—especially her chance meeting with Lawrence. The magical serendipity of Paris seemed to be following her home.

As the plane lifted off, she gazed out the window, excitement bubbling up inside her. She reclined in the comfortable seat, eager to embrace whatever coincidences and growth lay ahead. She couldn't wait to share everything she'd learned with Ethan.

Catalyst Two

Begin Within

"And the day came when the risk to remain tight in a bud was more painful than the risk it took to blossom."

~Anaïs Nin

After a magnificent lunch and a nap, somewhere over the Atlantic, Mirabel reached for the journal she'd bought at the Louvre. She'd never been one to write down her feelings. But now, with hours ahead and her mind on Paris, she felt a need to capture these thoughts before they slipped away. Opening the pristine pages for the first time, she let her thoughts flow:

- *Happiness is living with joy, love, and trust daily*

- *It's letting go of negativity and embracing possibilities*

- *It's seeing life as an exciting adventure full of hope and opportunity*

- *It means freedom from struggle and worry, recognizing that everything is okay*

- *It's about connection and seeing potential everywhere*

Her pen hesitated. Then, she added: *My caution with money has kept me from living this way. Fear dictates my decisions, always worried about not having enough. It's the opposite of what I want.*

Hours later, the plane began its final descent into San Francisco, she felt nervous about sharing her new ideas with her practical, money-focused husband. His Polish immigrant parents had instilled a strong work ethic and interest in financial success. Ethan managed their finances carefully, building wealth through wise investments and frugality. He took pride in the security he'd achieved for them through discipline and working hard at his tech marketing agency.

The shuttle pulled up to their home, and as Mirabel wheeled her suitcase to the door, her stomach fluttered with anticipation. She took calming breaths, reminding herself of her newfound clarity. This truth felt essential to her identity, and she owed it to both of them to express it, regardless of his initial reaction.

"I'm so happy you're home!" Ethan enveloped her in a long, warm hug and kiss. "Was it amazing?"

"Yes... in ways you can hardly imagine. Plus I got upgraded to first class on my flight home! It was divine!" Mirabel replied, kissing and hugging him back. Even in his familiar embrace, her mind was racing ahead to decisions already half-made. "I'm so happy to see you. The trip was life changing. And there's something important I want to discuss."

Ethan's brow furrowed as they sat down on the couch in the living room. "I'm listening. What's going on?"

She began sharing her trip's highlights, trying to capture the magic she'd found through Leila's eyes. Finally, she took a deep breath. "The thing is...my time in Paris opened my eyes," she said. "I saw how much of life we've been missing out on. We've let a mindset of frugality rule our choices, sacrificing presence for money and security."

Ethan's hand stiffened in hers, but Mirabel pressed on. "I know this may surprise you. But after a lot of thought I've come to see how we often play not to lose, rather than playing to win. I want to talk about changing this approach."

As she confessed to exceeding her budget in Paris, he pulled his hands out of hers. "I discovered a new way of seeing," she mused, barely registering his deepening frown. "Suddenly, I was noticing details and experiences I'd always denied myself before. It was as if Paris granted me permission to immerse myself in life itself."

Ethan's jaw tightened. She had to convey that her shift was more than a fleeting tourist excitement. "Before this trip, my splurges always caused guilt. It felt like I was doing something wrong." Mirabel reflected, missing how his shoulders had tensed. "But Paris... Paris transformed me. It shattered the barriers of anxiety I've been trapped by forever. For the first time, I was present. I savored each moment, free of my usual fears about money."

The etched lines on his forehead deepened. "Whoa, hold on a second," he said. "I mean, I'm happy you enjoyed yourself, but this sounds reckless." He ran a hand through his hair, agitation clear in the gesture. "We can't just ignore our financial responsibilities. You know the bills we have to pay every month just to live?" His eyes searched her face, confusion evident. "What exactly are you suggesting here?"

"Slow down... I'm not suggesting we start spending frivolously," she assured. "But when was the last time we embraced an experience for pure bliss, without obsessing over costs?" She described the decadent meals, the sunsets, and her conversation at the airport with Lawrence. "We can't just live to pay bills. There is so much more to life than that. I also want us to enjoy our life together!"

Ethan shook his head. "You're sounding like those hippies who throw caution to the wind. We have to be responsible adults. I'm sorry but we don't have much left after expenses each month. It simply wouldn't be smart to suddenly spend a lot more than we already do."

His words stung, but for the first time in a long time, Mirabel persisted. Her heart raced and her hands trembled, but she forced herself to continue. "So, trying to feel secure means we can't have any fun now? What's the point of living like that?"

She wrapped her arms around herself, her voice softening despite her resolve. "It's not just about spending money. It's about realizing that we've both been living in fear about money since we were kids. And yes, I'm terrified too—every time I buy something more than groceries, I hear my mother's voice warning me about ending up on the street. But that fear, that constant anxiety..." She met his eyes, willing him to understand. "We don't know anything other than that and it just isn't working for me anymore!"

An uncomfortable silence fell. Finally, he spoke, looking guilty and sad. "I want to support you. But I didn't experience what you did in Paris—a trip that was already a stretch for us. Remember how we agreed it was a one-time exception? How careful you needed to be?" His fingers touched his temple. "You promised you'd be careful!"

"I know, but—" she tried to speak but he interrupted.

"Look, I want to stop stressing and enjoy life more too. But what you're talking about doesn't work with our situation. I'm self-employed. My income isn't stable nor consistent. We need to stick to our budget, live within our means." His voice softening. "I don't know how to support what you're talking about here. It feels like Paris made you forget all the careful planning that got us this far."

She interrupted, "I appreciate your responsibility with money. But feeling less stress about money is about making choices with confidence." She took his hands and held them as she described Leila's self-acceptance and ability to adjust her spending for what's most important to her. "I want that for us—to stop doubting ourselves and each other." She held his gaze. "Our struggles hinder our joy and our love. I love you, and this could help us create so much more together."

His expression hardened as he pulled his hands away. "I love you too, but I don't think you're being realistic. You can't expect me to change everything because of some epiphany you had or because your friend said you should."

Mirabel couldn't take it anymore. She stood, her voice rising with frustration. "Do you even hear yourself? All you care about is money... and I've been right there with you! What about our happiness?"

As the argument escalated, she felt her jet-lagged mind spinning. Just hours ago, still high from her Paris revelations, she'd hoped he'd see her wisdom and embrace this new way of thinking. That naïve hope now felt almost laughable. A small voice in her head whispered, *Stop being so argumentative. Just let him have his way.* But the energy of the trip overrode that voice for the first time in a long time. She refused to back down.

He shot up from the couch and threw up his hands, pacing across the living room. "Of course I care about our happiness! But I also care about our future!" He spun back to face her. "Someone has to be responsible here!"

"Responsible? More like controlling!" she scoffed, moving to the opposite side of the room. "You treat me like someone who can't be trusted!"

"Well, can you blame me?" he shouted, his hands clenching into fists. "Every time I give you freedom, you go overboard! Remember that shopping spree a few years ago?"

"That was one time!" she replied, her body rigid as she jabbed a finger in his direction. "I bought an expensive handbag. It wasn't a good decision, and I learned from it, but you won't let it go!"

"I'm trying to protect us," he replied. "I don't want us broke and struggling."

"But we're not really living!" Mirabel's anger continued to flare. Then, forcing her body to relax, she crossed the space between them and took his hand, her tone shifting to a controlled, pleading note. "I appreciate everything you've done. But can't we find a middle ground? A way to be responsible and enjoy life more?"

He looked down at their joined hands, his jaw clinching before he pulled away. "I don't know. You think I'm happy being the bad guy?" he snapped, backing away and pressing his palms against his temples. "You think I enjoy worrying all the time?"

Despite her tendency to avoid conflict, she stood firm. She squared her shoulders and spoke with a strong, resolute voice. "Then let's find a better way! Let's work together to live well without risking it all."

"And how do you propose we do that?" Throwing his arms wide, his tone dripping with skepticism. "One fancy trip to Paris and now everything we've built isn't good enough?"

"I never said that!" she shouted, frustration boiling over. "But at least I'm trying to grow, to change. At least I'm not afraid of wanting more."

"I'm not afraid," he snapped back, his body coiled tight as he spun away from her before whirling back. "I'm being realistic. I'm protecting our future."

"But what about our present?" she asked, taking a step toward him. She was feeling desperate, but wanted to challenge his assertion.

They stared at each other, heavy breathing filling the space, as their arguments hung between them. Mirabel saw the hurt and frustration in Ethan's eyes, mirroring her own. She wanted to reach him, to make him understand. But the chasm between them felt wider than ever.

"I can't do this right now," Ethan said, his shoulders slumping with weariness and defeat. "I need some air." He grabbed his keys with jerky movements and strode toward the door, steps rigid with tension.

Mirabel watched him go, tears stinging her eyes. She collapsed on the couch, drained and hopeless. This was exactly what she had hoped would not happen. How had they gotten here, letting their differences drive them apart?

As the door closed with a final click, sorrow overwhelmed her. She curled up on the couch, the fight draining out of her. Ethan's words about responsibility weren't wrong—they'd worked so hard for their security. But as she sat in the hollow silence, she ached for what they'd lost along the way. There had to be a way to honor their careful planning while rediscovering joy together.

She realized it was time to confront the long-festering issues. A small voice questioned her strength, but she clung to hope. Fear coiled like a serpent in her chest as doubts crept in. What if Ethan couldn't handle the truth that things weren't so great for her? Or worse, what if he decided to leave for good? Their relationship had become a brittle facade, and she couldn't keep pretending. This surely wasn't the life she had envisioned for herself, but despite the terror threatening to paralyze her, Mirabel knew she had to act.

Drained from the emotional turmoil, her body still fighting Paris time, Mirabel dragged herself to their bedroom. She grabbed her favorite soft blanket and a pillow from their bed, her movements heavy and slow. Back on the couch, she curled up as tears slipped silently down her cheeks. The jet lag finally won, pulling her into an uneasy sleep. She wouldn't know until morning that Ethan had come home that night, or about the difficult conversations that lay ahead.

Mirabel's first day back at work was a study in divided attention. As she walked into the office, an immediate sense of unease washed over her—something felt off, though she couldn't quite identify what. The familiar surroundings seemed subtly altered, as if viewed through a distorted lens.

Yet even as she tried to puzzle it out, her mind kept circling back to Ethan and their tense conversation after her return. Their exchange played on repeat in her head, his words clashing with her newfound perspective.

She found it nearly impossible to concentrate on her work. Her eyes were on her computer screen, but her mind oscillated between the office's strange atmosphere and her conversation with Ethan. Each competing thought tugged at her focus, leaving her mentally exhausted and struggling to engage with her tasks.

A sudden knock on her office door jolted Mirabel from her melancholy feelings. She looked up to see Malik, one of her team members, standing in the doorway, his expression troubled. "Hi! Welcome back." He paused. "I need your help with the project we've been working on. It didn't go well while you were gone. There were some communication problems. I'm trying to fix them," he said, his voice laced with concern.

She tried to focus on Malik's words. "Okay. What's going on?" she asked, straining for a neutral tone.

He fidgeted nervously. "Our biggest competitor beat us to market with a similar product. They were already outperforming us, and now they'll dominate. I wish I knew what their secret was," he admitted, deflated.

She pushed aside her personal issues, focusing on Malik and their upcoming deadline. "Malik, what's stopping you from adjusting the plan with this latest information?" she asked.

He looked down. "After we got the news, the team sort of lost our momentum. We could really use your help with some adjustments to our plan."

She responded firmly despite her own wavering confidence, "Malik, I trust your abilities. You and the team need to own this problem and find a solution. The best leadership I can offer is letting you figure it out yourselves."

She watched him nod his head. His shoulders looked tense as he left her office, and she could tell he had lingering doubts.

Why does a team of professionals seem to need my help with just about everything...? she thought to herself, massaging her temples.

Her thoughts immediately turned to Aisha. What would her supportive boss think about the team's latest crisis? Unlike Mirabel's past supervisors, Aisha saw her potential. She praised her strategic thinking and pushed for her promotion to management. That made the prospect of disappointing her even more daunting.

Adding to her stress, she'd seen the email in her inbox about Rebecca, a key team member, who had quit without notice while she was on vacation. The news gnawed at her. Had she missed the warning signs? Failed to see her team member's unhappiness? Her stomach knotted as she imagined facing Aisha. Even after three years of success, Mirabel still strived to be the perfect manager her boss envisioned.

The joy from her vacation felt distant now. Staring at Rebecca's resignation email, something felt off. Her hand drifted to her phone, hovering over her sister's contact. They hadn't spoken much since Sarah started her new job. But as quickly as the thought came, she dismissed it. Her sister was finally thriving—the last thing she needed was to hear about Mirabel's management troubles.

A few days after the unsettling meeting with Malik, Mirabel met her friend Tanya at Ocean Beach. As they strolled down the shore, the late afternoon sun and gentle waves eased her mounting pressures. These monthly walks had been their ritual since college, 15 years of friendship distilled into sea spray and honest talk.

Tanya was exactly who Mirabel needed. She had a gift for perspective, honed by years of advocacy work at a women's health nonprofit. Her passion shifted hearts and minds as she helped marginalized women take control of their lives and their pregnancies.

Unlike Mirabel, Tanya never hesitated to speak up for what mattered. After Ethan's reaction to her Paris revelations, Mirabel needed that kind of courage. Her husband's response had left her feeling alone in her marriage, but here with her best friend, she could share her awakening without fear of judgment.

"Tanya, I have so much to share," she began, her words tumbling out like waves rushing to shore. "My trip to Paris was eye-opening. I had several experiences that caused me to see myself in a new way, and what I saw wasn't very pleasant."

Tanya turned to her friend, raising both eyebrows. "What do you mean?" She gave an encouraging smile, ready to lend a supportive ear.

Mirabel took a deep breath before continuing. "I realized that I've been playing life safe, always worrying about money and not taking risks. It's like I've been holding myself back from embracing life's pleasures. And now I think I resisted these thoughts before in order to keep the peace with Ethan."

Tanya drew back slightly, as if seeing Mirabel anew. "That way of thinking can be tough to break free from. What made you realize all of this?"

Mirabel's eyes lit up as she recounted her favorite moments in Paris, describing how liberating it felt to set aside her usual money worries. She turned from the waves to face Tanya. "Remember those weekend shopping sprees in college? When I'd max out my credit cards and then panic about rent?"

"Oh yes," Tanya laughed. "Like that time you bought three identical dresses because they were 'on sale.'"

"And now look at me—I agonize over the smallest things." Mirabel's smile faded slightly. "That's what hit me in Paris. There I was, sitting at this gorgeous café, actually afraid to order a second croissant. Me, a successful executive, counting euros like I was still that broke student." She drew a deep breath, her voice softening. "In that moment of clarity, I recognized this fear of 'not enough' had been silently dictating my choices. Something about that city... it sparked something in me. Made me wonder what life could look like if I loosened the reins on my frugality."

"That sounds promising," Tanya said.

Mirabel kicked at a piece of driftwood. "When I told Ethan about this revelation, he just... shut down. He started listing the financial mistakes I'd made in the past, like I haven't changed at all."

"You two have been on the same page about money for so long."

"Right, but Ethan doesn't support this. He's afraid I'll become irresponsible with money. It hurts that he doesn't trust me, but I know I need to do this for myself."

Tanya leaned forward, her expression softening. "I hear you, and it's a powerful realization you've come to. But you know, each of us walks a different path. You've had your own mix of struggles and privileges that brought you here. Have you considered how Ethan sees things? My own experience tells quite a different story."

Mirabel kicked off her sandals, letting her feet sink into the cool sand as they walked. "Okay. I'm trying to keep an open mind here. But maybe you can help me. How do you think tougher backgrounds shape people's relationship with money and progress?"

Tanya was quiet for several steps, watching a seagull dive into the waves. "It's not straightforward," she began carefully. "I've seen this from multiple angles. I've felt the weight of limited resources, growing up in a discriminated community. And now, through my work, I witness these struggles daily."

They stopped walking, turning to face the ocean. The wind was picking up, blowing their hair all over.

"Breaking free from that cycle? It's like climbing a mountain in flip-flops. It's not only about lacking money. It's the constant stress of not feeling like you are enough, the invisible scars of trauma. Mirabel, these experiences... they don't just make it hard to build wealth. They chip away at your self-worth, erode trust, and can make dreaming big feel like a luxury you can't afford."

Mirabel listened intently, her heart aching for the struggles that so many people faced. "I can't imagine how challenging that must be. How do you help people navigate those obstacles?"

Tanya smiled. "In my work we meet people where they are, focusing on empowerment, education, and community. We teach practical skills but also work on healing past wounds and nurturing hope."

"That's beautiful," Mirabel said softly, the words catching slightly in her throat. "I'm trying to do that for myself too—moving forward and believing I'm worthy of more."

They walked in silence, their feet sinking slightly in the cool sand. A patch of sunlight broke through the marine layer, briefly warming their faces before disappearing again behind the shifting fog.

Finally, Tanya squeezed Mirabel's hand. "You are worthy," she said, her voice firm but gentle. "And when we heal ourselves, we light the way for others to do the same." She paused, considering. "Perhaps Ethan's struggling with his own personal traumas about money?"

"You're right," she said softly, feeling a spark of understanding ignite. "His parents' immigrant experience shaped so much of his relationship with money. Thank you for helping me see this differently." She straightened up, her voice growing more determined. "I want to work through this thoughtfully, not from a place of ignorance or reaction."

Tanya was quiet for a moment, then said, "You know, life can be challenging for many of us. We all face different obstacles, whether it's personal struggles, societal expectations, or just the everyday pressures of life. It's natural to feel discouraged sometimes when we're constantly faced with difficulties or messages that make us doubt ourselves."

"I don't want to ignore the struggles others face, including Ethan. But I also feel this deep desire to break free from these feelings of lack. I want to prove to Ethan and to myself that I can do this responsibly."

"I work with communities that are treated unfairly every day. For many of them, getting by is a struggle. The idea of living like you're in Paris all the time does seem pretty unrealistic." Tanya's doubt was clear in her voice.

"I want to help people move past that constant feeling of not having enough, no matter where they come from or what their life looks like."

Tanya sighed. "Your heart's in the right place, but we're up against beliefs that run generations deep."

The words hung in the air as they made their way back towards their cars.

Mirabel finally said, "It just feels so unfair. We're told that anyone can succeed if they just work hard enough—that it's all about personal responsibility and making the right choices. But that's not the whole story, is it?"

Tanya nodded. "No it isn't. That's why our work at the nonprofit is so important. We're trying to fix these systemic issues—to create a fair society where everyone has a genuine chance at a good life. Even those who 'make it' with good jobs and degrees still face subtle discrimination and daily stresses that wear them down. Education and money can't fully shield people from unfair treatment. We're fighting for something bigger: a world where your race and background don't determine your future, where success means more than money. It's about dignity, respect, and true opportunity for everyone."

Mirabel felt a mix of sadness and determination as they arrived back at their cars. " get why you had concerns about my new outlook. It's not a simple fix for everyone."

Tanya leaned against Mirabel's car and said gently. "I hope I didn't dampen your spirits. I just wanted to paint a fuller picture, you know? Life's tapestry is... complex."

Mirabel stepped forward, enveloping her friend in a warm embrace. "No, I get it. I'm at the beginning of a long road, but I'm eager to learn... to grow. Your honesty means the world to me."

As Mirabel reached for her car door, Tanya's eyes lit up. "Oh! Before I forget—we've got our annual fundraiser coming up. Any chance you and Ethan could make it this year?"

She hesitated, weighing her personal challenges against her desire to support her friend. "I'll do my best to work it out," she promised while at the same time remembering how much Ethan detested these sorts of events.

"You're the best!" Tanya called out, already heading to her own car. "Love you, friend. Keep me in the loop!"

Settling into the driver's seat, Mirabel let out a sigh. The conversation replayed in her mind, a mix of revelations and complexities. That familiar sadness crept in—the one she couldn't quite name and didn't want to examine. She opened her music app, letting the algorithm choose her next song, as Taylor Swift's song "All Too Well" came on.

Her hands tightened on the steering wheel. Tanya's words had stirred something deeper than the usual anxiety—something raw and demanding to be heard. The music called to her as she merged onto the highway. With the sun beginning to set, she realized she had an unexpected challenge ahead. Her journey was just beginning, and what lay beneath the surface wouldn't stay buried much longer.

A week after returning from Paris, Mirabel sat warming her hands around her morning coffee mug. The Saturday silence felt different from the strained quiet that had filled their house all week. She and Ethan had perfected a dance of avoidance. They shared space but not conversation. They ate dinner together but barely met each other's eyes. He'd tried to respect her need for distance, keeping his questions about Paris locked behind pressed lips.

In the gentle morning light, her mind was troubled. The idea of feeling inspired and happy—concepts that had once filled her with hope—now felt like a burden. Her conversation with Tanya and Ethan's dismissal had left her in a state of deep unease.

She felt the urge to abandon her quest for joy grow stronger, with brief moments of lightness feeling like cruel teases. As sadness welled up, she focused her thoughts on what was missing, what wasn't enough.

How can you be so focused on your own fulfillment when you have duties to your family and work? A harsh voice within her demanded. *Ethan is struggling. Mom has money problems. Your team is failing. And you're worried about enjoying life more? Selfish.*

Her heart sank under the weight of her own self-recrimination. The familiar darkness crept in, threatening to swallow her whole. She had learned that a good woman puts everyone else first: her husband, her family, her work. That's what she should do: focus on being a supportive wife, a dutiful daughter, a dedicated employee and manager. Push down her own needs and ignore the growing emptiness inside.

What she'd thought was a sudden dissatisfaction had actually been growing deeper and darker for years. Each day, she went through the motions, checking boxes and meeting expectations, trying to ignore the void within. But living half a life while yearning to feel alive wasn't working anymore. And now, even her guilt couldn't silence her desire to live more fully, to feel free.

The morning light shifted across the patio. She sat with conflicting thoughts. She remembered the journal she'd started on the flight home from Paris and went to retrieve it from her bedroom.

As she reread her notes—something stirred within her. She'd written about wanting to stop being trapped by fear, about finding a way to honor both her responsibilities and her own happiness.

Mirabel knew this new mindset would shake the foundations of everything she'd built—her carefully crafted habits, her comfortable routines, her careful relationships. But for the first time since returning home, she felt excitement along with the old fears. Despite the uncertainty churning in her stomach, something fierce and determined had awakened within her.

She closed the journal. "I need help putting this into action," she whispered to the empty patio. "I can't do this alone."

She considered her options. Leila would understand. She'd seen glimpses of this in Paris. But her colleague had taken on a massive website overhaul when they got back. The last thing Leila needed was Mirabel's existential crisis on top of 60-hour work weeks.

Then she remembered Lawrence. He'd gone from cynical to centered with the help of a mentor who'd helped him shift his perspective. Mirabel felt a glimmer of possibility thinking maybe this was the guidance she needed.

Feeling motivated, she dug out his card and sent him an email seeking his advice.

Lawrence, I enjoyed our talk. I've been thinking a lot about it since then. But I think I need some help applying these ideas to my own life. Can we talk on the phone so I can ask you a few questions? Thanks, Mirabel.

She nervously hit send, hoping Lawrence could point her in the right direction.

A few hours later, Lawrence replied enthusiastically. He was happy to hear about her interest and agreed to a call later that day.

"Great to hear from you, Mirabel!" Lawrence said as they began. "How can I help?"

She poured out everything that had happened since getting home. The hard talks, the unsettled feelings at work, the lack of joy, her scattered thoughts. She even joked about quitting her job, leaving her husband, and traveling the world. But then her voice cracked as she admitted she wasn't being realistic.

When she paused to breathe, he spoke up. "I'm sorry it's been so overwhelming. It sounds like you've learned a lot! That's good."

"Good? It doesn't feel good at all," Mirabel said. "I feel awful. My only options seem to be going back to how things were or leaving everything behind. That's crazy. I don't know why it's so hard to bring what I was feeling in Paris back into my life!"

"You're right, those are extreme," He agreed. "But what if you met my coach? People call her the Money Catalyst, though she'd never say that herself. Like a catalyst that changes one substance into another, she can speed up changes that might take years, or never happen at all. She could help you sort through these questions and find clarity. She's very selective about who she works with, but if she takes you on, I think she could help you find your way forward. How does that sound?"

"The Money Catalyst? That sounds intriguing. But why is she so selective?"

"Maya isn't your typical coach," He explained. "She blends financial expertise with intuition. That's how she got the nickname. Having achieved financial independence before 45, she now only works with people she feels genuinely called to help. After twenty years as a lawyer, she understands firsthand the demands of a high-pressure career. Her uniqueness is that she can quickly find what's holding someone back. She certainly did that for me. She helps break down the invisible barriers that keep people stuck in their old patterns. She's living proof that you don't have to choose between success and happiness."

The hope of working with a coach who understood both money and the feelings she was having made Mirabel's heart race. "It's exciting but also a little scary," she admitted. "I'll do whatever she tells me."

Lawrence made a sound of disagreement that carried through the phone. "Maya will guide you, but you decide what works best. Your path is unique to you. You must discover what that means for you."

"I think I understand." She hesitated, then added, "I'm worried about time. How long does it take to work with Maya?"

"Maya only works with fully committed clients," He noted. "She wants to empower them to choose a prosperous, fulfilling mindset, not to create dependency."

"That sounds really good," she replied. "Knowing there's a structure is reassuring."

After exchanging contact information and warm goodbyes, she didn't waste any time. She crafted a heartfelt email to Maya, explaining her Paris transformation and her desire for change. Maya's response came a few hours later, and they scheduled their first video call the very next evening.

When they connected, Mirabel felt instantly at ease. Behind Maya's shoulder, a beautiful white orchid caught her eye, its petals glowing in the sunlight from the window. She noticed a few self-help books on the shelf behind Maya, arranged neatly against the beige walls of what looked like a home office.

Maya kept smiling, letting Mirabel know she was there without speaking. The light from the window cast a gentle glow on Maya's face. Mirabel felt a surge of hope and determination. She was ready to embrace the journey ahead.

When Maya spoke, her voice was warm and direct. "Hi Mirabel, I'm glad to meet you. You mentioned a few things in your email, but I'd love to know why you want to work with me."

"Sure," she said, her voice trembling. She paused and took a deep breath. "Recently, I've discovered a different way of seeing life. Instead of always worrying about what could go wrong, I want to embrace what could go right. I had this amazing sense of freedom in Paris right before I met Lawrence, but I'm not sure how to keep it. I'm terrified of falling back into my old habits of criticism and self-doubt."

Maya sat with this, taking in what Mirabel had shared. "Tell me more about this feeling you experienced in Paris," she said. "What felt different?"

"I felt... lighter," she explained. "Like I didn't have to constantly calculate every decision. But maybe that's because I was on vacation?"

Maya nodded. "I'm hearing that you've had a glimpse of a different way of being—one with less worry and more trust. But making that shift permanent feels overwhelming." She paused.

Maya asked another question, "Tell me Mirabel, are you happy?"

"Well, if you had asked me a few weeks ago I would have said yes..." she paused. "But now I don't know anymore. I feel like I should be happy. I mean, I have so much." She gave a small, hollow laugh. "If I'm honest, I'd say, maybe not. Paris awakened me to what real happiness feels like. I can't remember ever feeling so free and filled up with joy. Maybe I'm kidding myself that I could feel that way all the time...?"

"You know," Maya replied, "what you're describing—this shift—it's a natural transition. Once you get a taste of real happiness, if it means enough to you, you're going to want to keep it going. But you're right, it takes time to change." Her voice was warm with encouragement. "The good news is that you've already taken the first step, even if it was only for a moment in Paris."

Mirabel wiped her eyes. "But how do I hold onto that? Everything feels so different now that I'm back home."

Maya took a slow breath. "I see this pattern often in my work. We live our lives through a lens of fear always bracing for what might go wrong. But there's another way to live, one that doesn't ignore challenges but faces them with grace and trust." She watched Mirabel take this in. "When I was practicing law, I drove an old Toyota while my partners bought new sports cars. But I wasn't just being frugal—I was learning to find joy in choices that aligned with my values."

"I want to believe that's possible," she said, "but I can't imagine not comparing myself to others. How did you get past that?"

Maya settled into her chair, her warm eyes holding steady on Mirabel's face. "Many people say they want to live an abundant life but they don't even know what that means. I started by asking myself a different question: 'What would truly make me happy?' Instead of looking at what others had, I focused on understanding my own definition of success. It wasn't easy—I still caught myself comparing sometimes. But gradually, I realized that my colleagues' choices weren't bringing them the contentment they hoped for."

She paused thoughtfully. "True abundance isn't about magical thinking or ignoring real-world responsibilities. It's finding the middle way—between planning for tomorrow and living today, between being practical and staying open to joy. When I finally understood that, comparing myself to others lost its grip on me."

"That sounds... nice. But how do you get there? I'm constantly worried about money, about the future. How do you just... stop?"

"You don't simply stop," Maya said, leaning in with gentle intensity. "This transformation unfolds naturally, but I've discovered ways to accelerate it. Through years of working with clients, I've identified eight Catalysts that fundamentally shift how people relate to money." Her eyes lit up. "Together, they form the word 'Abundant'—and you've already experienced the first two Catalysts on your journey here."

Mirabel's eyebrows rose. "I have?"

"Yes," Maya said, her voice warm. "I'll pull it up on my screen and walk you through it. The First Catalyst—Awaken to Possibility is what happened to you in Paris, and through meeting Lawrence. Sometimes we need life to shake us awake, to show us there's more than the path we're walking. Your trip disrupted your usual patterns, giving you a glimpse of what else might be possible."

The 8 CATALYSTS

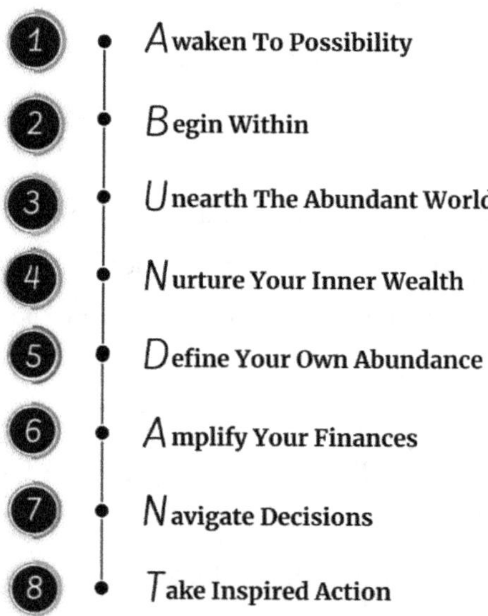

She let that sink in. "The Second Catalyst—Begin Within is where you are now. It's that restless feeling, that inner knowing that something needs to shift. You're realizing that real change starts here," she gestured to her own heart, "before it can manifest in your outer world."

"I'm guessing that explains the disagreements I've been having with everyone," Mirabel said sarcastically. "Even with myself."

"Exactly. It's like the ground shifting beneath your feet. But that discomfort? It's necessary. It leads you to the Third Catalyst—Unearth the Abundant World."

"What does that mean?" Mirabel asked, leaning forward.

"It means discovering that you're not just a victim of circumstances," Maya explained. "You have more choices than you realize. But first, you need to become aware of the unconscious patterns driving your decisions—patterns that keep you cycling between feelings of not enough and enough.

Mirabel shifted in her seat. "That sounds... scary and enlightening."

"It can be," Maya acknowledged with a soft smile. "But once you see the world through this new lens, everything changes. It's like turning on a light in a dark room—suddenly you can see what was always there." She let the metaphor settle.

Mirabel remembered how Lawrence had shared something similar when they spoke at the airport.

Maya continued, "That clarity prepares you for the Fourth Catalyst—Nurture Your Inner Wealth where you turn inward at a deeper level. We don't face our fears until we're ready. This step is about building that strength, discovering who you really are beneath all the 'shoulds' and 'musts.'"

"Okay, I get that. And then what?" she asked.

"Then comes the Fifth Catalyst—Define Your Own Abundance."

"This is when you get to decide what abundance means for you, not what advertising or society or anyone else says it should mean."

"That's... different from what I expected," Mirabel replied with a chuckle. "I thought this would be about vision boards and manifesting—you know, putting pictures of dream houses on a board and hoping they appear."

Maya shook her head, a knowing smile playing at her lips. "No vision boards here. This is about something much more practical—learning to see what truly matters to you and what doesn't. When you strip away all the things you think you're supposed to want, what remains? That's where life truly begins."

"When do you actually focus on money challenges?" she asked.

"That's the Sixth Catalyst—Amplify Your Finances," Maya replied. "But by then, money becomes what it should be: a tool to create the life you want, not the source of your security or worth."

"Got it, that sounds very helpful," Mirabel noted.

Maya continued, "The Seventh Catalyst—Navigate Decisions is about developing a reliable process for making choices that align with your values. And finally, the Eighth Catalyst—Take Inspired Action is about finding the courage to act on those decisions."

Mirabel was quiet for a moment, absorbing it all. "But what if I can't do it?" she finally asked, her voice small. "What if the old worries come back?"

Maya's response came with a gentleness that made Mirabel's shoulders relax. "That's a natural concern. The goal isn't to eliminate all worries—that's not realistic. Instead, we build new habits. We learn to spot old patterns and choose new responses. We start small with what feels possible right now and grow from there."

She took a deep breath. "I want that. I want to learn how to worry less and trust more. But..." she trailed off, then looked at Maya. "So once you learn this new way of thinking, does the old way of looking at life go away?"

"Think of it more like learning a new language," Maya said, her expression soft. "The old language remains, but over time, you gain greater fluency in the new language. Your old perspective might always be there, but it won't be the only way you know how to see things anymore."

"That makes sense," said Mirabel, feeling her heart skip a beat. "So when can we start?"

Maya sat back, her gaze and tone steady. "Okay... To be clear, we're talking about a few months of challenging those old beliefs and building new patterns. Some days will get messy. Some days will be very uncomfortable. Are you ready for that kind of journey?"

Mirabel didn't hesitate. "Yes. I can only imagine this won't be easy, but I'm ready. This process feels like just what I need."

Maya studied her hard, as if she was reading a complicated book for the first time. "Something about your determination reminds me of myself years ago," she shared. "Okay, let's do it. We can find an evening this week to start. I think we have important work to do together. You'll have my formal proposal in your inbox tonight—investment, contract, the eight Catalysts, everything you need to review before we start."

"Perfect," Mirabel said with a grin. Maya's acceptance had touched something inside of her. Even though a small voice whispered doubts about such a momentous leap, she knew in her bones it was perfect.

For the first time since their argument, Mirabel felt a sense of resolve as she approached Ethan the next evening after dinner. She had been mulling over how to bring up the subject of working with Maya. Mirabel knew this talk was key—important for her growth and their relationship.

As they sat on the couch, she took a deep breath and began, "Ethan, there's something important I want to tell you. I recently learned about an amazing coach named Maya. I am sure that working with her could help me."

Ethan's eyebrows drew together while the corner of his mouth twitched upward, caught between interest and wariness. "A coach? What kind of coach, and what exactly would you be working on?"

She gathered her thoughts before responding. "She's a money coach. She used to be a lawyer actually, but now she helps people create fulfilling lives while being smart with their money. It may sound strange but I feel that working with her will help me grow. It will also improve our lives together. I'll cover the costs with some of my recent bonus from the project at work."

Ethan furrowed his brow, processing Mirabel's words. "I'm not thrilled about the idea of you spending money on this, but I can see how much it means to you. As long as she's not teaching you how to spend more money, I suppose I'm open to it," he said with a chuckle.

The sound of his laughter hit her like a physical force. For years, she'd cycled through this same sort of response from Ethan with things that were important to her. Leaning on her sister and friends when things got tough between them. She needed more than venting and temporary comfort. She needed someone who could help her and Maya could be that person. Yet here was Ethan, reducing it all to a joke about money.

"Ethan, I don't appreciate your patronizing tone," she exclaimed.

"What? I said it was okay!" Ethan retorted, completely missing the point.

She stood up, her resolve strengthening. "You're not listening and you do this to me all the time. I don't need your permission or understanding. I'm doing this for my growth—with or without your support." She was done with the pattern of endless discussions that left her exhausted but unchanged. This was her chance for real transformation.

Her voice cracked with emotion as she delivered her final words: "I'm working with Maya. That's not up for discussion."

Without waiting for a response, she turned and left the room, her emotions threatening to overflow. As she walked away, she felt a shift. Despite the uncertainty ahead, she knew she was finally prioritizing herself. If Ethan couldn't accept this new dynamic, he'd just have to adjust on his own.

As the sun began to set, Mirabel got ready for her first session. Sitting in Ethan's home office, which she sometimes used, she made sure Maya could see her clearly on the camera. "I've been looking forward to this all day," she said with a smile.

Maya nodded. "Me too. It's great to see you again. Thank you for filling out my paperwork and answering my questions. I'm happy you started meditating with the instructions I sent you." She paused, then added, "You know, when I first left law, despite having everything planned financially, I realized I had no idea how to truly live. I'd spent so many years doing what others expected that I'd lost touch with what I most wanted."

Mirabel leaned closer to the screen. The computer's light made Maya's face glow. She was surprised by this admission from someone so centered now.

"It took years of exploring—meditation retreats, mindfulness, mentors, and much trial and error—all before I developed the Eight Catalysts. All of these helped me get where I am today," Maya continued.

"That's why I'm excited about our work together. I know this path of transformation because I've walked it myself."

Mirabel absorbed Maya's words. "Meditating has already helped me feel calmer," she said. Her eyes glanced at the reddish-pink orchid behind Maya, as if drawing strength from its beauty. "It's been so useful to pay attention to my thoughts! But I'm definitely easily distracted."

Maya smiled, her eyes bright with genuine enthusiasm. "I'm so glad you're willing to try this. What I want to share with you today is something I've developed specifically for deepening mindful awareness—it's a practice that helps you stay present, especially when facing difficult challenges." She leaned forward slightly, her gesture welcoming and encouraging. "I call it A.W.A.K.E. Let me walk you through it—I'll send you a detailed diagram and we can explore each component together."

Mirabel opened the file. The image showed a circle with five steps: Awareness, Willingness, Appreciation, Kindness, and Embodiment.

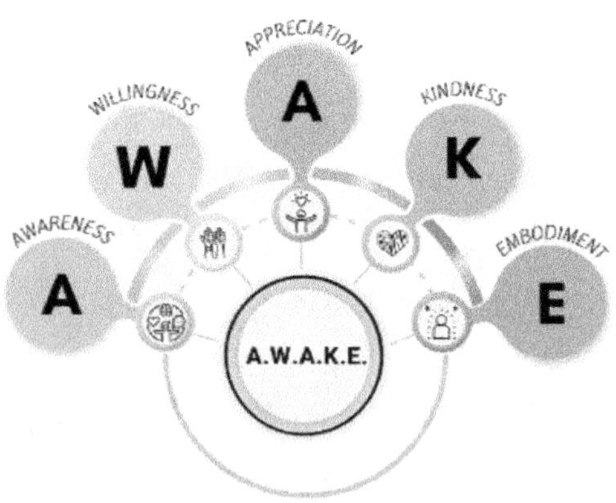

"A.W.A.K.E. is designed to help you calm your nervous system. It's easy for anyone to learn," Maya explained. "It ties together practices for your mind, body and emotions. The steps are so straightforward, even a

10-year-old could follow along. The idea is to go through each of these steps at least once a day as part of your daily practice, so they become a mental habit."

"I love that," she said. "Keeping things simple helps me. Excited to learn how it works."

"Okay we'll start with A for Awareness which means getting grounded and centered. Noticing your breath, your bodily feelings, and your thoughts," said Maya. "Imagine you're a detective investigating what's happening inside yourself in the present moment. Start by focusing on your breath for a few minutes. Then sit quietly and notice what you're thinking and feeling, without judging it. You may notice things you're holding onto inside that aren't helpful, so pay attention to all of it."

"I see what you mean. It's like watching my thoughts instead of being caught up in them. Just a few days of meditating and I'm already noticing a difference."

"Next we have W for Willingness," Maya replied. "This is where you check in with yourself with curiosity. Asking yourself, *'Am I open to receiving life and other people as they are?'* or *'Am I wishing for things to be different?'* Willingness is about approaching life with a curious and open mind to see what is wanting to be learned from life itself."

"Willingness is a pivotal moment in a person's life," Maya continued. "It's the moment when you choose to forgive others, understanding that people are doing their best given their unique circumstances. It's when you decide to accept what has happened without resistance, embracing the present and letting go of the past. When you become willing to shift your perspective, your entire outlook transforms."

Maya paused, allowing her words to sink in before continuing. "Embracing willingness means you're open to releasing the thoughts that hold you back and weigh you down. It's about liberation from the burdens of resentment, anger, and regret. By cultivating a willing mindset, you create space for growth and healing. Willingness unlocks the door to a more peaceful life."

"That's definitely a perspective shift," Mirabel said, scrunching her nose and giving a slight shake of her head. The memory of feeling suffocated by Ethan's control crept back. "I'll be honest—this one's going to be hard for me. When I don't feel supported, I tend to jump to conclusions and shut down." She got quiet for a moment. "What you're saying makes me think of flowing downstream with the current instead of struggling against it. I like that idea, but I'm going to need help getting there."

Maya nodded thoughtfully. "You bring up a good point. This isn't about letting people off the hook or not holding them accountable for how you wish to be treated—that's very important. The shift is about not being pulled astray by your emotions. It's about staying fully present to what's happening, with compassion for both yourself and others, while clearly stating what matters to you."

"Okay," Mirabel said slowly, "that makes sense to me."

"Next comes A for Appreciation," said Maya. "When you take time to reflect on what you're grateful for, it's like shining a flashlight on the good things that light up your life. This practice connects you to joy and your best self."

Mirabel nodded thoughtfully. "That's a beautiful analogy. I try to practice gratitude but want to do more. Do you think it could help me feel more confident about myself and my choices?"

"Definitely," Maya replied. "Just take a moment each day to remember one thing you're grateful for. You'll gradually become more attuned to the energy of gratefulness and all the ways it supports you."

"Then there's K for Kindness. This means pausing to consider how you can show more compassion to yourself and to others. It's about actively choosing kindness throughout your day, remembering that everyone—including you— is doing their best. Forgiveness is part of this practice. You'll understand how it all connects as we work together."

"Wow! That is beautiful," she said. "I can see how self-kindness would help me feel better inside, and how extending it to others would strengthen my relationships. So, the final step, Embodiment—how does that work?"

Maya explained, "Embodiment means internalizing the positive feelings from the process. It's about tuning into your mind and emotions, then carrying that positivity with you. This fosters a mindset of self-trust, joy, and love-based actions. It's like tending a garden," she mused. "At first, the soil might be rocky, but the more you nurture it by removing obstacles and planting seeds, the more beautiful it becomes."

Mirabel's eyes lit up. "Oh, I love that metaphor." She paused, imagining how this might bloom in her own life and then added, "So the more you practice A.W.A.K.E., the more naturally your mind returns to that state of joy?"

Maya nodded, her voice gentle. "Yes, the more you practice it, the more it will help you slow down and meet life where it is."

"I think I'm starting to understand."

"The goal is to help you self-regulate in daily life," Maya continued, "so you can pause and avoid reacting impulsively to whatever comes your way."

"I can see how this could help me." Mirabel's shoulders dropped as she sighed. "I've been so reactive with Ethan lately."

Maya nodded in understanding. "That happens. This is a way to gradually neutralize those patterns you've fallen into. Taking a moment to breathe before responding to upsetting situations can help. You can reflect and be more patient with yourself. Each time you reject a negative thought, you rewire your brain. You also build self-trust. The steps of A.W.A.K.E. guide you through this inner shift."

"As we close for today, I want to share one more thing," Maya said gently. "This practice will help you find peace within yourself, but it doesn't mean accepting behavior that harms you. You can work on your own healing while still setting healthy boundaries. Sometimes the most authentic choice is to step away from situations that don't serve your highest good—whether that's physically or emotionally. Your wellbeing matters, in all its forms."

"Thank you for explaining that," she replied, her brow furrowed slightly. "I guess Ethan and I are going through pretty normal relationship stuff, but I never thought about these distinctions before. It's hard to tell sometimes... when we're just having a tough conversation versus when we're falling into patterns that might be harmful."

Maya studied her for a moment, a knowing smile touching her lips. "Remember, this is a process. Take it one step at a time and be patient with yourself." She wrote a note to herself. "I'm sending you some journal prompts to explore before our next session that will help you do this."

Mirabel smiled gratefully. As she signed off, she felt a newfound determination coursing through her. The world outside her window seemed a little brighter, a little more full of possibility.

Catalyst Three

Unearth The Abundant World

"Look closely at the present you are constructing: it should look like the future you are dreaming."
~Alice Walker

Over the next few days, Mirabel included A.W.A.K.E. in her meditation practice in the morning and before bed. She also reviewed the mindfulness and journaling questions Maya had sent:

Mindfulness and Journaling Practice

Close your eyes and take a few deep breaths.

Connect with your younger self. This innocent, wise part of you who holds your deepest truths.

Then ask yourself: "When in your life did you feel most secure and complete? What made you feel that way?"

Once you've explored that memory, stay connected to your younger self. Then, ask: "Beneath your desire for more money and success, what do you really want to heal?"

Mirabel began the exercise, taking deep breaths to get centered. As she connected with her younger self, she started by asking, "When in your life did you feel the most secure and complete? What made you feel that way?"

Memories flooded in with surprising clarity. Saturday mornings meant pancakes with her father—golden stacks she'd drown in maple syrup while he spun stories that made her feel like the center of his universe. Whenever she got sick, he'd appear beside her bed with ginger ale and her dog-eared books, his deep voice bringing characters to life until her eyes grew heavy and she drifted off to sleep.

The realization hit her with gentle force: those early morning moments, that time of her life, were when she had felt most secure and complete. It wasn't the pancakes or the stories—it was how her father's love had created a cocoon of safety around her. His presence had made the world feel manageable, predictable, and full of possibility.

But when she turned eight, the magic began to crack. Hushed arguments leaked under doorways. Slammed doors punctuated dinner times. Tension filled their house, making it hard to breathe.

Then came that day when she bounced home from school, eager to tell her father about scoring the lead in the class play. Instead, she found her mother standing at the kitchen sink, washing dishes that were already clean. Her father's coat was missing from the rack. The house felt hollow, like someone had scooped out its insides.

Her mom, Sheena, never explained. She pressed her lips together and scrubbed harder whenever Mirabel asked about Daddy. Alone to make sense of her shattered world, Mirabel concluded, with her eight-year-old heart, that she hadn't been good enough to make him stay.

Her father called a few times to try to explain, but she was too upset to listen to him. Sensing her distress, he gradually began to distance himself until he no longer contacted them. Her mother, consumed by her own pain, concentrated on practical matters. There was no therapy or support to help her. Only her mother's constant worry about money and managing without her father's income.

Mirabel was the oldest. She felt responsible for her younger sister Sarah, who was only four at the time. She stepped up to help her mother, trying to fill the emotional void left by their father's absence. However, this left little room to deal with her own pain and feelings of abandonment.

It left a deep wound in her heart. She came to believe that the people she loved could leave at any moment. Little Mirabel concluded that to feel safe, she had to play it safe. She needed to work hard and sacrifice her own desires. She also had to avoid rocking the boat. This belief system would go on to shape her life choices and her relationship with money.

As she moved to the next question—"Beneath your desire for money and success, what do you really want to heal?"—a profound realization emerged. Her younger self craved love, attention, and validation—things that money couldn't buy. Her throat tightened. She saw her emotional poverty after her father left. She had tried to fill the void for her mom and sister and not worry about herself.

Her father's face floated in her memory, and Mirabel's pen faltered mid-sentence. A familiar ache spread through her chest. Her vision blurred as tears gathered, remembering how his pride had transformed her world. Every "that's my girl" and proud smile had made her feel like she could conquer anything. In those moments, wrapped in his love, she had felt invincible.

The truth spilled onto the page: more than anything else in her life, she longed for that time before he left. That was when she had felt whole, secure in her place in the world. For all these years, she had been holding onto a child's hope for his return.

Her ambitious pursuit of success suddenly made sense. Every promotion, every achievement, every raise, was an attempt to recreate that feeling of being truly seen and valued. Yet the emptiness remained, despite her success. A profound sadness settled in her bones as she recognized how this desolate void had shaped her adult life.

Her writing slowed to a near stop as an even harder truth emerged: her fear of abandonment had silenced her. The thought of expressing her needs, of driving away those close to her, had become a quiet prison of her own making.

Her tears fell freely now, dotting the page as the final words took shape. The truth lay exposed in ink—raw, uncomfortable, but undeniably real. And in that reality, lay the first seeds of healing.

She set down her pen, stunned by how much had poured out of her from just a few simple questions. Years of buried pain and understanding had broken free like a dam giving way. She let the waves of emotion wash over her—grief for the little girl she'd been, anger at what was lost, and relief at finally understanding. When Ethan came to check on her, she shook her head. "I need to be alone right now," she whispered, her voice thick with tears. She needed to stay with this younger version of herself, to hold space for all the feelings she'd never allowed herself to feel.

In the quiet aftermath, she held her realizations close like precious, fragile things. The rawness of it all left her feeling more vulnerable than she'd felt in years. Though uncertainty clouded her mind, she knew that she couldn't go back to hiding these parts of herself.

As she reached for her journal to capture her thoughts, a strange uneasiness stirred in her chest. If my drive for money and success had been to fill the void left by my father, what did I truly want? Her hand trembled as she closed the journal. Perhaps it was time to stop fighting against the current and see where it might carry her.

It had been a little over two weeks since her return from Paris, each day a slow unfolding of tension and revelation. Now, on a Wednesday evening, Mirabel sat in Ethan's office chair, grateful he was at his weekly basketball game. The past few days had been an emotional whirlwind—her raw conversation with Tanya, the growing silence between her and Ethan, and finally, her decision to reach out for help.

When Maya's face appeared on the screen, Mirabel exhaled. Maya's steady presence made her feel safe enough to explore these newfound truths.

"Good evening," she greeted. "I've been working with those journaling exercises you suggested, and..." She gave a shaky laugh. "I wasn't prepared for what came up. A few days ago, I ended up crying on my couch for hours—the kind of crying I haven't done since I was a little girl."

Maya's eyes softened with understanding. "That's often how break-through moments feel. When we finally let ourselves see what we've been carrying..." She left the thought hanging, creating space for Mirabel to share.

"It was like opening a door I'd kept locked for decades," Mirabel said, her hand moving to her chest where the ache still lingered. "I always thought my drive for achievement was about being successful, being secure. But it goes so much deeper than that. When my father left..." Her voice cracked, surprised by how fresh the pain still felt. "I was eight, and suddenly our whole world changed. Not just financially, but emotion-ally. I became this little girl who thought if she just worked hard enough, sacrificed enough, kept everyone else happy enough..."

She took a steadying breath as tears began to well up. "I've spent my entire adult life chasing a feeling of security I lost that day. Every achievement, every promotion, was an attempt to fill this void. I wanted to prove I was worthy of staying for. I learned to silence my own needs, convinced that speaking up might drive people away."

Maya nodded, her presence anchoring Mirabel in the vulnerable mo-ment. "I am sorry for what happened to you when you were eight. That must have been very difficult for you."

She sniffled several times, trying to hold back her tears and spoke softly. "I find myself trying to fill those empty spaces all these years later. But

I'm starting to see how some of my attempts at fulfillment are actually holding me back. Right now, I'm caught between caring for others and acknowledging my own needs."

Maya's eyebrows lifted slightly as she leaned closer to the screen, her expression like a doctor who'd just spotted something significant. "Mirabel, that's a big realization," she said, nodding. "Recognizing these patterns is crucial. It takes real courage to face these hidden truths."

Behind Maya, an orange orchid swayed in a soft breeze as Mirabel felt a wave of relief wash over her. "It's been exhausting," she admitted as tears ran down her cheeks. "I've lived for others, hoping their joy would somehow become mine."

Maya's voice gentled. "You're not alone in this, Mirabel. So many people get caught trying to find themselves through others' validation. But lasting joy comes from within—from learning to value ourselves, imperfections and all."

Mirabel cried for a few moments, the weight of recognition pressing against her chest. "I want to learn how to do that. How to actually put myself first sometimes without feeling selfish. I just... I don't know how."

Maya nodded; her eyes warm with understanding. "You're already taking the hardest step—seeing these patterns and choosing to change them. We'll work together to build new habits, set healthy boundaries, and create a better relationship with yourself."

Mirabel's forehead creased. "I also have to admit..." She bit her lower lip, searching for the right words. "These popular books I've been reading, they make it all about money and getting more. But that feels different from what you've been sharing."

Maya's shoulders relaxed as her face brightened with recognition. "I can see why you're grappling with this," she said, a small smile playing at the corners of her mouth. "There's so much more to living fully than accumulating money."

Mirabel nodded, feeling a sense of anticipation.

"Some people think that having a lot of money means you can do, buy, and say what you want. But this does not always make you feel happy and fulfilled. Buying things only makes you feel good for a short time. After you get something, the good feeling often goes away."

Mirabel flashed on the designer handbag she had splurged on. The initial thrill had faded, and now the bag sat unused in her closet.

Maya leaned forward and said, "Inside each of us, there's an infinite source of power that connects us to everything. It's like a never-ending source of happiness and confidence. When we learn how to access this power, we feel like we have everything we need."

For Mirabel, this sparked memories of times she had compromised her values for financial gain, leaving her feeling empty. She recalled her childhood passion for art, wondering about reconnecting with that creative spark.

"When we're not in touch with our true feelings and desires, we might chase after things thinking they'll make us happy," Maya explained, her eyes fixed on Mirabel. "But if those things don't match our values and passions, they won't bring lasting happiness."

Mirabel thought of her grandmother, who had grown up poor in Mexico but refused to let circumstances define her. She embodied Maya's philosophy of harnessing inner power to create positive change, facing adversity with an unwavering spirit. This helped Mirabel understand that it wasn't about magical thinking—it was about believing in human potential and taking inspired action.

"True abundance isn't about expensive possessions," Maya said softly. "It's about the experiences you have, the connections you make. These stay with you forever, and you can give them any meaning you want. That's why choosing experiences over things is more likely to cause you to feel fulfilled."

Mirabel recalled a fulfilling camping trip with friends, recognizing that her most precious memories were rooted in shared experiences rather than possessions. Maya's words offered a perspective she hadn't found in many of her books.

"To get started on the Third Catalyst—Unearthing the Abundant World, I want you to spend time thinking about who you really are," Maya said. "This will help you to become more confident in yourself. You can start this by writing down 'I am' statements. Let's start this together, and then you can keep working on it this week. How does that sound?"

"Great, I'm ready." Mirabel grabbed her pen and wrote her statements, then read aloud, "I am powerful... I am loved... I am strong... I am smart." She paused and then added. "I am creative. I am kind and fierce. I am generous. I am a nurturer. I am always learning. I am curious."

Maya asked, "How does it feel to recognize these parts of yourself?"

"Good. It's helpful because these are things I know about myself but also forget," Mirabel replied.

Maya smiled, "These 'I am' statements are not just words; they're reminders of your unique qualities and strengths. By accepting and honoring these parts of yourself, you're accessing your potential and honoring the wealth that's already within you."

She continued, "You'll find that your self-worth and confidence grow. You'll start to trust in your ability to create what you want and you'll be more likely to make it happen."

Mirabel nodded, feeling stronger.

"Continue with these concepts in your journaling practice," Maya urged. "Be mindful of how your outlook evolves. Meditate every day.

Observe your actions. Remember, practicing what we're exploring together helps you move forward."

Mirabel ended the call feeling inspired and full of energy.

After the session, Mirabel needed space to process. She went to the kitchen and filled the kettle, finding comfort in making tea. The soft padding of footsteps made her look up. Ethan stood in the doorway, his expression uncertain.

"Hey," he said. "I've been thinking about everything lately, and I probably haven't been as supportive as I could be." He moved into the kitchen but kept his distance, respecting her space. "I guess I felt threatened by all these changes you're going through. And honestly..." he let out a slow breath "I'm not sure I really understand what's happening with you."

Mirabel watched him, noting how he struggled to find the right words. It was rare to see him this vulnerable.

"I know it's not fair to try to control you," he continued, meeting her eyes. "I'm sorry for that. I want to do better, be more supportive. I just... I want you to know that."

Mirabel stirred her tea. His words hung in the air between them, heavy with unspoken emotion. Part of her longed to go to him, to lose herself in the familiar comfort of his arms. But another newly awakened part, knew she needed this time apart. She needed it to find herself again. She needed to untangle the knots of their past.

She met his gaze. She saw the sincerity in his eyes and the love that still burned beneath their recent conflicts. "I appreciate your apology," she responded. "And I understand feeling threatened. My time in Paris, the things I'm learning about my past, my work with Maya—you're right, it's changing me. But I need you to trust that my love for you hasn't changed, even if I need some space right now."

She reached out and squeezed his hand briefly. "I'm not going anywhere. I need some time to sort through what I want, who I am apart from us. Can you give me that?"

He touched her arm, trying to pour all his love and commitment into that small gesture. "Of course," he said, his voice thick with emotion. "Take all the time and space you need. I'll be here, whenever you're ready."

He cleared his throat, blinking back the dampness in his eyes. "I'll let you finish your tea in peace. But Mirabel..." He paused, making sure she met his gaze. "I love you. Don't forget that." With a small, sad smile, he turned to leave even though she could feel how every part of him ached to stay by her side.

A few days later Mirabel had a dream that brought back a powerful memory. When she woke up, the scene played out in her mind like it had just happened yesterday. It was a strong reminder of what she had buried deep inside but needed to heal. This experience had made her feel like she wasn't good enough.

She jogged onto the soccer field, scanning the sidelines for her dad. He never missed her games. Her mom sat in the bleachers with her sister, giving a small wave. The pain of their dad leaving still showed on their faces. Mirabel kept looking, heart racing. Maybe he was just late from work or stuck in traffic. He'd be here soon to cheer her on and give her a post-game hug, she told herself.

The referee's whistle pierced the air as she took her position, her eyes darting to the sidelines between plays. With each passing minute, a growing distress settled in her stomach. A slow realization dawned painfully: for the first time ever, her dad wasn't coming to her game.

As the clock ticked on, the absence became undeniable. A wave of sadness washed over her, too immense to process in the moment. Unable to handle the grief, she pushed it down, burying it deep inside as she forced herself to focus on the game.

When she woke up from the dream she was crying. She felt a surge of compassion as she reflected on her younger self. Now she could clearly see the sadness. Unable to secure what she yearned for most—her father's attention and love—she had been forced to seek alternative sources of fulfillment.

This childhood loss had cast a long shadow over Mirabel's life, subtly shaping her choices and relationships. It drew her to Ethan, whose stability offered a refuge from uncertainty. In her quest for security, she often sacrificed her own desires, believing it necessary to avoid further hurt.

This self-protective instinct had become a silent barrier. It kept her from voicing her true wants and needs, from reaching for her full potential. Like an invisible hand, she had allowed this childhood wound to dictate her adult life, choosing safety over growth, comfort over challenge. It was only now, as she began to unravel these long-held beliefs, that she realized how much of herself she had kept hidden, even from herself.

Still unsettled by the dream, Mirabel carried its emotional weight with her throughout the day. At work, she ran into Leila and, seeking some normalcy, provided an update on her decision to hire Maya.

"So far, she's given me a lot to think about. It's changing how I see things, especially how I see and treat myself," she shared, her voice steady despite the lingering unease from her dream.

Leila's interest piqued. "I'm so glad you found someone who can help you. Please, tell me more."

Mirabel took a deep breath. "It's... transformative. Maya recently taught me to use 'I am' statements to reshape my self-perception. I am supposed to affirm them daily."

"Wow, that's great!" Leila exclaimed with genuine enthusiasm. "How does it feel to be making these changes?"

A small smile spread across Mirabel's face. "It's liberating, honestly. For the first time, I'm truly getting to know myself and my innermost thoughts. I'm more aware of that harsh, critical voice in my head, but I'm also learning that perfection isn't a prerequisite for feeling self-worth."

Leila's eyes crinkled at the corners as she smiled. "It's so crucial to believe in yourself. I'm happy for you."

As they began walking down the office hallway together, she felt a wave of gratitude wash over her. "I'm beginning to learn what true wealth really means..."

Lost in thought, Mirabel nearly missed Leila's goodbye as they parted ways at the elevator.

Later that evening, Mirabel sat down at her computer, excited to meet with Maya for another session.

Maya's face appeared, and as before, it brought a smile to Mirabel's face. Joy washed over her, she felt safe and trusting of Maya, a rare comfort she cherished.

Mirabel began to describe her recent dream and the changes unfolding in her life. Beneath her enthusiastic words, a subtle tension lingered.

"Maya, I've wanted to talk to you," she began, her voice a little hesitant. "I'm so grateful for everything. But I'm having some real concerns about my husband and his resistance to all of this..."

"While he didn't forbid me from working with you, I can sense his frustration. We're not on the same page. For weeks I've been sleeping on the couch because I can't get through to him and need my own space. I refuse to cave in as I have before. I used to believe his dismissiveness was justified, that I didn't deserve to be heard. But as I've started standing up for my needs, it's led to more conflicts between us. I struggle to embody this self-awareness around Ethan, so I withdraw instead of addressing our issues."

She looked at Maya with hope and vulnerability. "I was wondering if you could give me some advice on how to approach him. I want to be a better partner and not tell him he's wrong and I'm right. I know there has to be a way to communicate with him that brings us closer instead of pushing us apart."

She sat back, feeling a sense of relief. She knew her mentor's guidance would be invaluable.

Maya replied, "What you're describing isn't unusual. When we make changes in how we think about things, it can stir up a lot of emotion and resistance from our partners. I see this all the time. I can definitely help."

"For now, it would be useful if I understand more about your back-stories with money and any certain beliefs you were brought up with. Would you be willing to share more about that?"

Mirabel nodded and began sharing details about their lives. She explained that Ethan's parents were immigrants who worked hard despite having little money. Growing up with financial worries left Ethan afraid of being poor again. He was careful with money, using spreadsheets to track their finances. While not religious, he was interested in mystical ideas and often read books on mindset and building wealth. He had been investing in stocks since college.

"I have one sister, who is four years younger than me," she continued. "Our father left when I was eight, leaving our mother to raise us alone. Mom wasn't religious, so we never went to church or had any spiritual guidance growing up. I believe in God now, but it's not something that plays a big role in my life."

"Dad's abandonment affected me. It made me feel inadequate and distrustful in my relationships. As a result, I often defer to others rather than asserting my own needs." She explained. "Financial struggles were a constant in our house. My mother still grapples with money problems today. I started working at 14 to help out, which felt normal at the time, but looking back, I guess it was a lot for a kid to handle."

Her voice softened. "That fear of being abandoned, of not feeling safe—it's stayed with me since Dad left. I see now how I let Ethan control things just to maintain stability." She let out a small, bitter laugh. "The irony is, once my sister was grown and independent, I finally had more money of my own. But after years of feeling deprived, I went through this period of overspending. I worked hard to increase my income to cover my expenses, but then Ethan and I bought this foreclosed home 7 years ago." She shook her head. "The strain on our finances just gave him more reason to tighten his control over my spending."

Maya leaned forward. "As I listen to your story, I want you to remember something important: Growth takes time. Be gentle with yourself through this process." She let that sink in. "Our early experiences, especially around money and security, shape how we see the world today—and how we see ourselves."

Her voice softened. "Sometimes these experiences create parts of ourselves we try to hide away. Think of it like peeling back layers of an onion. Each layer we remove might make us cry, but it brings us closer to our authentic core. The shadow side holds our deepest fears—fear of failure, of judgment, of not measuring up."

Mirabel nodded slowly, recognition flickering across her face. "I never thought about it that way. Sometimes I catch myself holding back in meetings, not sharing ideas because I worry they're not good enough."

"That's it," Maya said warmly. "That self-censoring comes from the shadow side. But those supposedly 'not good enough' ideas? They're often the seeds of innovation. When we learn to embrace our whole self, including these shadows, we unlock our full creative potential."

"I want to share something with you," Maya said, a glimmer in her eye. "Check your email—I've sent you something" She smiled as Mirabel clicked to open it. "I created this description of a place called Scare City. It might help you understand how many of us have a scarcity mindset without even realizing it."

"Think of it like wearing invisible glasses that make everything seem scarce, no matter how much you actually have."

Maya's voice gentled. "And be patient with Ethan. Try to create positive experiences together. It's actually a good sign that he's noticing your changes—it could open the door to deeper conversations." She gestured toward the screen. "Would you read the Scare City description aloud? Sometimes hearing these words helps us recognize our own patterns."

Mirabel began reading.

Scare City: The World of Fear and Lack

Imagine waking up one day and finding yourself trapped in Scare City. It's a nightmarish place where fear and lack rule. It's like being stuck in an endless doom-scrolling session with your social feed, where every post reinforces your worries about the future. But instead of being able to put down your phone and disconnect, you hear the constant chatter of your own anxious thoughts.

The first thing you notice is a feeling like there's never enough, and that you'll never be enough. No matter how many resources you have, it's never satisfying. You're always focused on what's missing rather than what you do have. It's like wearing blinders. They only let you see deprivation and block out most of the opportunities.

Here, money carries dark meanings. It's vital for survival, and too little implies incompetence. The wealthy seem superior, as if money determines human worth. This irrational system breeds a society driven by insecurity, not potential. It warps views on wealth and poverty, fueling anxiety and self-doubt. People struggle to see their true value beyond finances and out-ward success.

In Scare City, many of the citizens grew up starved of love, acceptance and support, leaving them haunted by emotional wounds. Some try to fill the void through reckless spending, while others chase money, hoping it will validate their worth. But these strategies never satisfy the soul's craving for connection and wholeness. The people of Scare City keep looking for fulfillment in all the wrong places.

In Scare City, inequalities and discrimination are woven into the fabric of society, creating additional challenges for marginalized groups. The city's institutions, from education to employment to the justice system, are influenced by biases and prejudices that limit opportunities for growth. This oppressive environment not only hinders progress but also takes a toll on the well-being of those affected.

In Scare City, you have the illusion of choice, but having a choice between 250 different kinds of cereal is vastly different from having a choice about *the life you want to be living. The profusion of trivial options masks the lack of meaningful choices. This illusion keeps you trapped in a cycle of consumerism and distracts you from pursuing your genuine desires and aspirations.*

Living in Scare City becomes the only reality people know. They grow scared to leave, even for better opportunities, worried about leaving loved ones behind. Fear becomes a trap of the mind. Breaking free requires changing not just location, but how one thinks about fear itself.

Many in Scare City give up, accepting a life of painful mediocrity. Overwhelmed by anxiety, they feel powerless to change. Their only escape is dreaming about a peaceful retirement someday. But even this dream feels out of reach, like a mirage beyond a desert of hardship.

One day after living in Scare City for what feels like an eternity, something extraordinary happens—you have a sudden epiphany that completely transforms your perspective. It's like winning the lottery, but instead of hitting the jackpot, you've struck gold in terms of self-awareness and understanding.

In a moment of clarity, you see through the illusion of scarcity and limitation. You are not your fears or perceived flaws, but rather a being of boundless potential. Like a book with many chapters, your life contains both joys and sorrows. But you've lingered too long on the difficult pages. It's time to turn to a new chapter. You are the author of your story, free to write the future you desire, unconstrained by past experiences.

With this newfound understanding, you decide to buy a one-way ticket out of Scare City. You pack your bags, leaving behind the scarcity mindset and embracing the truth that you have everything you need within you.

As you board the train to a new life, you can't help but chuckle at the absurdity of having remained in such a strange place for so long. With a

*smile on your face and a spring in your step, you wave goodbye to Scare City,
ready to embrace a life of true abundance.*

Mirabel paused when she finished, feeling overwhelmed with emotion. The description mirrored her life, triggering memories of fear and insecurity. She realized living in Scare City was like being locked in some sort of mental prison.

"Why didn't anyone tell me I could free my mind from scarcity?" Her voice barely above a whisper. She wasn't looking at Maya on her screen. She was gazing into the middle distance. She felt raw and tinged with a mixture of both wonder and regret.

Maya's eyes filled with compassion. "This reaction you're having? It's exactly why I call these stages Catalysts," she said, leaning forward. "In chemistry, a catalyst creates a new pathway that transforms molecules permanently—they can never return to their original state. That's what discovering Scare City does to your consciousness. Once you see how deeply this mindset has shaped your reality, you can't unsee it. The activation energy has been reached." She gestured as if mapping an irreversible reaction. "Your mind has found a new, more efficient way of operating, and like a transformed molecule, there's no going back to the old configuration. This discomfort you feel? It's the catalyst doing its work, breaking old bonds so new ones can form."

Mirabel felt a cocktail of emotions swirled within her. Anger simmered beneath the surface—anger at the years lost in Scare City. Yet simultaneously, hope blossomed in her chest. This conversation hinted at a freedom she hadn't known existed, whispering of possibilities beyond the constant grip of fear.

Her eyes reflected both exhaustion and awakening. "I see now how my past has burdened me," she said, her voice gaining strength. "And what becomes possible when I begin to release these fears."

"Watch for the breadcrumbs," Maya said softly. "They've always been there. When you truly change, reality has no choice but to follow."

Maya suggested they take a break so Mirabel could take a short walk and then come back to dive into the second part of the discussion.

Grateful for the pause, she stepped outside, the crisp air a welcome change. As she began her walk, her mind buzzed with the insights about scarcity. Turning a corner, her thoughts drifted to areas of her life she had yet to examine. *What other blind spots could I uncover? And how would these revelations affect my life?*

With each step, Mirabel felt she was walking—not just through the neighborhood, but towards a version of herself she had yet to meet.

When they came back to the call, Maya said. "I'm going to read something that will feel like a meditation. Close your eyes, let the words wash over you, and pay attention to how your body responds. Allow yourself to be filled with warmth and compassion."

Living in the Abundant World

In the Abundant World, you wake up each morning feeling a deep sense of peace and contentment. You know that peace comes from within, not from others, and you trust in yourself and the universe to keep you secure and grounded.

Even when things don't go as planned, you adapt and remain resilient in the face of uncertainty. You understand that change is a natural part of life, and you embrace it with an open heart and mind. Your strength and flexibility let you navigate any challenge. You know that every experience is a chance to grow and learn.

The Abundant World is a realm of true choice, where you have the freedom to create the life you desire. The level of abundance you experience is directly proportional to how much of your innate power you tap into.

Here you can shape your reality according to what's most important to you. If you find yourself unsatisfied with your job, you have the capacity to change it. If you wish to increase your financial abundance, you can make it happen. If your relationships or living situation no longer serve you, you possess the power to transform them.

In the Abundant World, your choices carry profound significance, and you have the flexibility to align with your deepest desires and aspirations. As you go about your day, you experience a sense of equality and oneness with all of humanity. You understand that everyone's needs are met and their unique gifts are valued.

Here, you know that unconditional love originates from self-love and extends outward to create true community based on giving, empowerment, and shared resources. You feel a deep connection to others, knowing that what affects one affects all.

In the Abundant World, you have become skilled at giving to yourself. You know how to save energy. You understand that thriving does not require wearing yourself out. It also does not need more willpower than is natural or comfortable. By nurturing yourself and respecting your own boundaries, you create a sustainable and fulfilling life.

Living here you accept that everyone, including yourself, is doing their best. You appreciate the unique role that each person plays in the grand tapestry of life. You forgive easily. Letting go of past resentments feels like a bird soaring in the sky. Love is the strongest force in this world, and you feel it everywhere you go.

You tap into endless energy, like a tree with roots sunk in fertile soil. You experience this energy as a boundless spring of potential. Gratitude fills your heart, unlocking the door to abundance.

Your imagination and creativity flourish, bringing life to your existence.

In the Abundant World, you are thriving, connected, and alive. You wake up each morning eager to see the magic and wonder of this world. You know that you are a key part of the beauty that surrounds you.

Maya paused.

Mirabel sat in awe, hope blooming in her chest. The description resonated deeply, articulating a truth she had always sensed but never fully grasped.

After a few moments of silence, Maya's voice emerged with the quiet certainty of hard-won wisdom. "In twenty-five years of walking this path, I've not just glimpsed the Abundant World—I've lived in it. It is not always consistent, but I know what is possible when we align with our deepest truth and life's flow."

Maya leaned forward, her eyes bright with conviction. "This isn't just positive thinking or manifestation tricks. It's a fundamental shift in how you experience reality itself. When you first touch it..." She paused, searching for the right words. "The Abundant World can become your sanctuary, not just in your mind, but in your very being. In that space, your desires aren't future maybes—they're alive in you right now, pulsing with possibility. As you learn to dwell there, your consciousness transforms, and your outer world has no choice but to follow. The path requires dedication, yes, but I've watched this process unfold too many times to doubt its power. This isn't theory to me anymore—it's as real as the chair you're sitting in."

"I want to imagine myself living here every day. Thank you."

"Before we wrap up I know Ethan is weighing heavily on your mind, my suggestion is to print out these descriptions of Scare City and The Abundant World and leave them where he can read them too. You never know what could open him up."

"Thank you, that is a great idea."

When the meeting ended, Mirabel felt both clear-headed and excited. She knew she needed time to process everything, but her thoughts kept drifting to Ethan. Though he was practical about money, he loved exploring ideas that expanded his mind. Maybe, just maybe, this could be exactly what they both needed to grow together.

Catalyst Four

Nurture Your Inner Wealth

"When I dare to be powerful, to use my strength in the service of my vision, then it becomes less and less important whether I am afraid."
~Audre Lorde

A week after her last session with Maya, Mirabel stood at the kitchen counter, preparing a salad from the vegetables spread before her. The cherry tomatoes gleamed under the pendant light, while cucumber slices lined up like pale green coins. The tension in the room was palpable—three weeks of sparse communication with Ethan had left their normally comfortable kitchen feeling like contested territory.

As he approached, she noticed a few printed pages in his hand. She'd taken Maya's advice and left a printout for him to see.

"Hey, I noticed these on the kitchen counter." he said, tentatively.

Mirabel glanced up, meeting his eyes briefly before returning to her vegetables with a tightened jaw. She would let him start the conversation.

"They look interesting," he said. "I assume they're from Maya. I looked them over."

She nodded but kept her focus on the vegetables, the steady rhythm of her knife against the cutting board filling the space between them. The silence was a choice now—not awkward, but deliberate. She let it speak for her.

He leaned against the counter next to her, watching her, careful with his words. "I wanted to talk to you about something I read recently," he began, his tone gentle, almost pleading. "A friend recommended this article called 'Acres of Diamonds' by Earl Nightingale. I printed it out and think it offers some insights about our situation."

She paused, looking up at him. "What's it about?" she asked, her voice softer than usual.

Sensing an opening for a deeper conversation and connection, Mirabel stopped her preparation. The tension was easing between them for the first time in weeks. She took a deep breath, grateful for what felt like being on common ground for a real conversation.

"It's about an African farmer," he began, his voice filled with emotion and his eyes fixed on Mirabel. "He sold his farm to search for diamond mines. But he found out later that the farm he sold was one of the most productive diamond mines on the continent. The moral is that we often fail to recognize the riches and opportunities that are right in front of us, in our own 'acres of diamonds.'"

She turned to face him, wiping her hands on a kitchen towel. She relaxed and softened. "I appreciate you taking the time to reflect on this," she said. "I agree that we need to be more creative and resourceful. But I also need you to care about what's important to me."

"You're right," he acknowledged, his eyes almost teary. "I haven't been helpful. I'm committed to having more open-minded conversations with you."

He handed her the pages, his hand brushing against hers, a silent apology. "Here's the full article if you want to read it. I'd be curious to hear your thoughts."

She took the printout, a small smile tugging at her lips, a glimmer of hope in her eyes. "I'll take a look. Thanks for sharing this."

He nodded, relief washing over him as he saw Mirabel's smile. "This story reminds me to appreciate what we've got before seeking better things. It encourages me to look at our work and lives with fresh eyes, always seeking ways to improve and grow."

She leaned against the counter, considering his words, her body language more open than before. "I get what you're saying, but what does that mean for us? What opportunities are we missing?"

He reached out and took her hand, his touch gentle and reassuring. "I think we need to take a step back and really look at what we have here. Our home, our careers, our relationship—there might be more potential than we realize. Before we make any big changes, let's try to see our 'acres of diamonds' with new eyes and appreciate what we have."

She squeezed his hand. Her smile grew as the emotional wall between them began to crumble.

"I want to hear everything," he said. "About what you've been learning from Maya... about Scare City and The Abundant World, all of it."

She smiled. "Really?"

He nodded, then shyly added, "I know you've started dinner, but could I take you out? Tonight feels special."

Mirabel happily put her salad fixings back in the fridge.

Walking to their neighborhood bistro, hope flickered in her chest like a newly lit flame. He was finally ready to discuss how their perspectives had shaped their choices and their fears.

At their corner table, bathed in the restaurant's warm glow, she inhaled the rich aroma of garlic and herbs. It anchored her in the moment. The path ahead would reveal harsh truths and she felt ready to face them.

Mirabel had a disturbing dream the night before her next appointment with Maya. In it, she faced a quest to attain all the things she most wanted in life. Working with great gusto and immense effort, each time she achieved one desire, it pushed her toward the next.

However, with every win, she was forced to compromise her values. She had to harm others to get what she wanted. At the office, she stole an opportunity from a coworker, taking credit for their hard work. Another time, she was shopping for the perfect dress. But, when a woman showed interest in the same dress, Mirabel scared her away. Yet another time she wanted something she couldn't afford so she stole money out of her mother's wallet to buy it.

Things kept getting worse. She lied to get a lot of money that wasn't hers. On a project, she knew her actions would hurt the company's clients. But, she cared more about making money and looking good than doing what was right.

Each time she did something wrong, it felt even worse. But she kept going, thinking she needed to do these things to reach her goals. Eventually, she got everything she wanted: money, success, fame, and stuff. But instead of feeling happy, she felt empty and sorry.

In her dream, she saw this happening everywhere. People giving up their honesty and values to get more. Business people paying off politicians to ignore important problems they were in charge of fixing. Bosses paying workers as little as possible so they can make more. What stood out most was how she and the others had lost trust in themselves and their ability to make good choices.

She had everything she wanted. But in her dream, Mirabel felt very lonely and disconnected. She felt a big hole inside, even though she had achieved so much. When she woke up, she was crying.

She sat up on the couch, letting her dream settle in her mind. As she calmed her thoughts through meditation, clarity slowly emerged. She realized that chasing achievements at the cost of her values would never bring true fulfillment. The conversation with Lawrence echoed in her memory - she wasn't alone in learning this lesson.

As she prepared for work, her mind dwelt on her upcoming appointment with Maya and the lingering dream. Its timing felt perfect, as if the universe had delivered a crucial insight. The dream had changed Mirabel. It showed her new depths of humility and compassion for herself and others. These feelings welled up from her soul like a freshly discovered spring.

Then, out of the blue, a strange thought came to her. She'd always resented the ultra-rich, assuming they had it all, but now she felt a flicker of compassion for billionaires. Perhaps they too were trapped in their own cycles. They missed the simple truth she'd glimpsed. If the very wealthy understood what she now saw, might the world look different? But even as this understanding bloomed, it began to fade like morning mist. The dream's darker images crept back—compromise, moral decay, corruption, the slow erosion of values. She felt suddenly uneasy. Was she really so different from those she'd judged?

Seeking refuge from these thoughts, she turned on her playlist as she got ready. As Alessia Cara's "Scars to Your Beautiful" filled the room, its message of self-acceptance embraced her like a warm blanket. She swayed to the music. It reminded her to be imperfect, to hold both insight and doubt in her heart.

Mirabel stood in front of the bathroom mirror studying her reflection as a question arose. *How many times have I compromised my values while justifying it for success?* Each compromise over the years had seemed so reasonable. A white lie here, a blind eye there. Always the promise that once she "made it," she could do things differently. Her mind traced the path that had led her here, one justified concession at a time.

Standing there, stark realizations surfaced. *I wonder what hidden beliefs had been steering these choices? Were my own unexamined assumptions the real barrier and not my circumstances?*

As she reached for her purse, she was certain. She had a feeling that her next coaching session would crack something open inside her. She remembered Maya's early warning about the process being difficult, and now she understood why.

The following afternoon, Mirabel settled into her home office for her session with Maya. When her coach's smile appeared on screen, she found herself drawn to the orchid on Maya's desk—its green petals dotted with pink like tiny watercolor brushstrokes. As Maya asked about updates since their last meeting, she began sharing her dream and the revelation it had brought: how she'd been focusing on the wrong things all along.

"What a wake-up call!" Mirabel laughed. "My subconscious has quite the sense of humor—showing me how not to live."

"Your dream..." Maya said gently. "It speaks to exactly what we're exploring today. Society bombards us with this message—get rich, be happy. But how many wealthy people do you know who are truly content?"

Her smile faded and she looked down at her notes, avoiding Maya's gaze. "I get what you're saying, but... I've been chasing that bigger paycheck my whole life. How do I just flip a switch in my brain?"

Maya's eyes crinkled with understanding. "No switches to flip. Let's start smaller." She paused, letting the question form. "When I say 'wealth,' what's the first thing that comes to mind? Not what you think you should say—what actually surfaces?"

"Having enough money to feel secure, I guess," she answered. "To buy what I want, when I want it."

Maya nodded thoughtfully. "That's what many think. But it goes deeper than purchasing power. It's about cultivating a sense of having enough—and being enough—right now. That's where lasting happiness takes root."

"But doesn't money make that easier?" Mirabel pressed, leaning forward.

"Money solves practical problems," Maya acknowledged. "But I've worked with people who have millions and still feel scarce, still chasing happiness. Freedom is trusting you have what you need to create joy in your life. When you cultivate that trust, you use all your resources—including money—more wisely."

Mirabel sat back, absorbing this. "It's a lot to process. I've always thought more money would automatically mean more happiness. This feels... different."

"Take your time," Maya replied. "Now, let's explore limiting beliefs—thoughts that breed inadequacy. What beliefs might be holding you back?"

She thought for a moment. "The idea that I'll never have enough money?"

"Good example," Maya nodded. "How do you think you could question that belief?"

"I guess I could look at times when I did have enough, or even more than enough?"

"Excellent!" Maya beamed. "That's the kind of thinking that can replace limiting beliefs."

Maya leaned forward, her eyes intent on Mirabel. "Beliefs shape how we see the world. Our strongest beliefs often form early in life based on our experiences. Limiting beliefs act like blinders, making us focus on what we lack or what might go wrong. They push us to seek happiness from external things. These beliefs feel permanent, but they're not."

She paused, allowing her words to sink in. "Empowering beliefs work like windows—they open us to possibilities and inner strength. The key is that we can choose to develop these empowering beliefs and make them our foundation."

"Think of Scare City as a desert where struggling is normal. Each person faces sand dunes representing their limiting beliefs—obstacles telling them they don't deserve success or can't achieve it. The scarcity mindset and limiting beliefs reinforce each other. The desert makes us believe the dunes are impossible to climb, and the dunes convince us we can't escape the desert. It's a cycle fueled by feelings of not being enough."

Maya smiled. "Does that make sense?"

"Yes, absolutely," she replied. "It explains why they're so hard to change."

"Money is just a tool for exchanging value," Maya said. "When you stop fearing or chasing it, it loses its control over you. At the heart of it all is your mindset—how you think about money determines your relationship with it. The right mindset transforms everything."

"So it's about identifying and changing limiting beliefs, not just having more money?"

Maya nodded. "Our subconscious creates these beliefs to protect us, but they often shape our financial reality without us realizing it. These patterns can trap us in unhelpful cycles when we make money decisions."

"How do I start recognizing them?" Mirabel's brow furrowed.

"Look for patterns in your financial decisions that keep repeating despite your efforts to change. These beliefs helped you once, but now you can choose better ones."

"So not criticizing the beliefs, but first recognizing, then replacing them...?"

"Yes. When you approach money from an empowered perspective, you make choices that serve your well-being." Maya's voice softened.

"This takes time, but with practice, you'll see positive changes. It's about trusting your ability to create more."

"Now, let's take this understanding and apply it to your specific situation." She leaned forward. "I'd like you to choose one 'super sticky' limiting belief about money or even your relationship with Ethan. By super-sticky, I mean one that feels particularly difficult to shake off. We'll work on reframing it with A.W.A.K.E. and then I'll guide you through a process of consciously letting go of the belief."

Mirabel furrowed her brow in concentration. "The belief 'I am afraid to talk about my feelings with Ethan' is the most pressing and difficult one. It's not directly about money, but it affects our financial relationship."

"Excellent. This belief likely reveals how your past experiences with your father shape your current decisions."

"So, what I would like you to do now is have you close your eyes and breathe. Become aware of your body. This is the Awareness part of the process. Great. Now tune into your level of Willingness. How open are you to a new way of looking at your past?" Maya questioned.

Mirabel nodded and said, "I'm totally willing to see it differently."

"Great, now I invite you to connect with your most gracious and loving self. Take a moment to feel her presence within you. Notice the radiance and natural beauty surrounding you. Appreciate all that you are in this moment. Allow yourself to soak in all that loving and supportive energy."

Mirabel felt chills up and down her body as she let in Maya's words.

"Now, invite in the part of you that doubts yourself. Notice her thoughts, feelings, and the tension she experiences. Accept her state without judgment. Allow her feelings to exist. Then, let your most loving self speak to this doubtful part, with kindness. Share whatever comes to mind."

Mirabel spoke, "She's reminding me I'm more capable than I thought. The past is gone; it's time to shape my future. My past experiences don't mean I should fear abandonment. I need to discuss my feelings with Ethan. Share what happened with my father and my tendency to remain silent about my true needs. And that his control isn't necessary anymore. I really did want him to handle things I found uncomfortable, but that time has passed. I'm learning how to take better care of myself and will learn better money management skills too."

"Beautiful," Maya said. "You are validating who you are. This is true Embodiment. You had a limiting belief about not feeling secure which kept you from speaking up. When you are focused on this limiting belief—what does your life look like?"

She began to list what was coming to her. "I feel like a child. I don't trust life. I don't trust Ethan. I don't believe there are solutions for my problems. I spend a lot of time worrying about worst-case scenarios. I feel like I can't ask for what I want. I do not believe in myself...." She paused. "Oh my goodness. I had no idea all that was inside me!"

"Okay. Thanks," Maya replied. "Now get out your journal and a pen. Let me know when you're ready to continue."

Mirabel got her things and nodded.

"Great. Now please answer this by writing down what comes to you: Who do you become if you believe, 'I must tell Ethan the truth about my past, how I feel about money and his behavior towards me'?"

Mirabel took a deep breath and wrote what was coming to her, then read aloud, "I become a more powerful person, capable of making positive choices. I trust my voice and my worth. I can express my needs and desires, without fear of consequences. My thoughts and feelings matter, and I have the courage to share them honestly."

"Now, how does that feel?"

"Incredible!" Mirabel responded. "I feel powerful when I express my thoughts and feelings."

"Great job," Maya said, her eyes warming with encouragement. "You can continue this practice with other limiting beliefs later if you wish. Remember, it's important to do this with self-compassion and patience. Changing beliefs and habits takes time. It works because it's bringing mindful awareness into spaces that were hidden from view. Then they can be healed through your loving attention."

Mirabel shifted in her chair. "I love this process, thank you. I want to share something coming up if we still have time?"

Maya nodded her approval to continue.

"I'm still sleeping on the couch, keeping my distance with Ethan, but..." Mirabel let out a soft breath. "I'm starting to miss him. We had this nice dinner the other night, actually talked, but something held me back. I still needed time to process everything before falling back into old patterns."

Maya's face softened with understanding. "What I hear is that you're honoring your own timing," she said, letting her words settle. "When it comes to being more honest with Ethan, trust your instincts. Your inner voice will tell you when you're ready to open up, and when he's ready to listen. Don't force it. Let it unfold naturally."

Maya reflected on Mirabel's journey. "You know, up to this point in time, you've only seen yourself through the eyes of others, and for a very long time you kept conforming to that. Some people will do that their entire life—trying to do everything right for others." She leaned forward slightly, her voice gentle but firm. "What you're doing here is realizing that you can never win that battle. You're figuring out how to play life based on who you really are. This is what the Fourth Catalyst—Nurture Your Inner Wealth reveals."

Maya's words settled into the quiet. She straightened in her chair, her shoulders relaxing for the first time since they'd started talking. "Okay. I hear you." A small smile tugged at the corners of her mouth. "I feel like I can keep moving forward! Thank you!"

As Mirabel ended the call, she felt lighter, buoyed by new possibilities. The sunset streaming through her window caught her eye, awakening a sense of wonder she hadn't felt in weeks. She thought about her team at work, how they'd rallied through the recent setbacks in the project's development phase. She'd stepped back more than usual, letting them take the lead. Watching them rise to the challenge had validated her instinct to give them more responsibility.

Yet as she considered tomorrow's meetings, a familiar unease settled in her stomach. She didn't know it then, but her journey of self-discovery would soon collide with a harsh reality at work. It would test her new-found strength and the choices she'd made in the past.

A few days later, Mirabel woke up at 2:30 am. The moonlight filled the living room with a magical glow, like it was daytime. Sitting up on the couch, she enjoyed the peace around her. The full moon was so bright it rivaled the sun. It bathed the city in quiet stillness, as if the whole world was asleep except for her.

It had been over a month since her trip to Paris. In this luminous hour, she marveled at how things were shifting. The moonlight cleared her thoughts. Mirabel saw that with less fear, her world was changing.

Feeling more secure, she recognized her thoughts and values as her own. This lessened her need for constant validation from others. She had begun to reject outside influences on her mind, feeling stronger in her convictions. She was discovering how to create a culture of sufficiency that could ripple outward, touching everything around her.

Mirabel was also taking steady steps toward prioritizing her own identity over pleasing others. Though often challenging, she recognized it as an evolution unfolding day by day. One that felt worth the ups and downs along the way.

These gentle realizations danced in her mind as she surrendered to the peace that filled her heart. With each breath, she sank deeper into a restful slumber. She embraced the tranquility that enveloped her like the gentle moonlight.

The next morning, she awoke with a start, an unsettling feeling in her gut replacing her previous night's peace. The unease intensified during her morning routine. This nagging disquiet followed her like a dark cloud. It was an unwelcome visitor, clouding her as she commuted to work.

Once at her desk, she immersed herself in her work, hoping that the familiar rhythm of her projects would silence the unease that plagued her mind. Soon, however, the little focus she had was shattered by a summons from her boss, Aisha.

Mirabel was a swirl of hope and apprehension as she made her way to her office. Could this be about the promotion she'd been yearning for? Her boss was known for her razor-sharp clarity. She never wasted a moment on corporate niceties when truth would serve better.

Seeing Aisha's face, that flare of hope died. The arched eyebrow and tight corners of her mouth meant business. She sat behind her desk with the kind of quiet confidence that came from years of making tough decisions and standing by them. Her eyes, usually warm with approval, now held a gravity that made Mirabel's stomach drop.

Uh oh, this doesn't bode well, she thought, feeling her heartbeat start to speed up. She'd earned her boss' respect through three years of hard work. She'd basked in the rare praise from a woman who didn't give empty compliments. But that same directness now made Mirabel's palms sweat. Maybe the discomfort this morning was a premonition?

Aisha immediately dove in. "Mirabel, we need to discuss the marketing project you spearheaded a few months ago," she said.

"The idea you presented to the executive team—was it your brainchild, or did it originate with Rebecca? How did others contribute to its development?"

Mirabel felt the heat rising in her cheeks, a burning flush that betrayed her guilt. Why was she asking this now? Her mind raced between fight or flight—deny everything or run from the room. But Maya's voice echoed in her thoughts: The truth might hurt but lies will destroy you. These past weeks of working with Maya had shown her a new way of being—one where she didn't have to manipulate situations to feel secure.

Her boss didn't wait for her to respond. She continued, "As you know, Rebecca recently left the company. She wrote to HR after she left that it was because you took credit for her ideas, and she didn't feel appreciated. Rebecca was an asset to the company and losing her is a blow. I need to know what happened, so we don't lose any more great people."

Mirabel's throat tightened. Everything she'd worked for could vanish in the next few minutes. Her mortgage, her car payments, her whole life hung on this moment. Yet surprisingly, what scared her most wasn't the prospect of losing her job—it was the thought of betraying the person she was becoming. Maya had helped her see how her need to please others had twisted into something darker, something that hurt not just her but everyone around her.

Taking a deep breath, she admitted, "You're right. Rebecca came up with the main idea. Others contributed too. I shouldn't have implied it was mine."

The words felt like stones dropping from her mouth, heavy but somehow cleansing. She paused, gathering her thoughts. This honesty might cost her everything. But, lying would cost her something more precious: her integrity.

"I'm glad we're discussing this. I worried my actions caused Rebecca to leave. She is talented, and I hate to think I contributed to her leaving. I've been thinking about what I could have done better. When I tried talking to her a few months ago, she didn't say much. So, I'm thankful this is coming out now."

Aisha nodded, lips pursed and jaw clenched. "Rebecca left because she didn't trust you as her team lead. That made her doubt the process and the company's values. She took her ideas and talents elsewhere. If this is true, we need to make sure it doesn't happen again." She cocked her head to the side and squinted. "I'm curious: why did you do it?"

The question hung in the air. Six months ago, Mirabel would have crafted a careful response, something that would paint her in the best possible light. But now, Maya's guidance resonated within her: The truth isn't pretty, but it's where healing begins.

"I guess I wanted people to think it was my idea," Mirabel admitted. "I feared I wouldn't get ahead if others received the credit. I've recently been finding it more difficult to get ahead in this company, so I thought that was what I should do. I now know that was wrong."

Mirabel knew she had to fully come clean. The work she'd been doing with Maya gave her the courage to be vulnerable. "I've been rethinking how I see myself as a leader," Mirabel started. "I understand now that true success isn't about claiming credit. I was stuck in a loop, driven by fear of not measuring up. I've been paying attention to how I need to change to be a better manager. I know this isn't how I want to advance in this company."

For the first time since Mirabel walked into her office, her boss' face relaxed and softened. "I'm pleased you're taking responsibility for your mistake." She paused, then asked, "So what would you do now?"

Mirabel considered her response with great care. "Well, first, I wouldn't repeat my actions," she began. "I've come to understand that being a good leader means helping my whole team succeed. It's not about seeking personal recognition." She took a deep breath before continuing. "So, if Rebecca had come up with that idea today, I would make sure she got the credit she deserved. I'd have her help present it to you and the executives. The success of every team member matters."

Aisha studied her for a long moment, and Mirabel met her gaze, feeling a flutter of hope beneath her nervousness. Everything hinged on this moment.

Finally, her lips remained pursed as she spoke. "I want to be honest with you Mirabel. I appreciate your response and I want you to know how serious this is. You've done great work at the company. So, when my boss asked me about this, I told him I wanted to see your response. I wanted to know if you would own up to your mistake before deciding what to do. I told him I believe in you and your reaction today supports that."

Her back straightened as she sat up in her chair. "I've also noticed some changes since you got back from Paris. Leadership is a journey, Mirabel, and sometimes our worst mistakes teach us the most valuable lessons. I think you're trying to become a better leader and I'm willing to help you make that transition."

Her voice took on a firmer edge. "But let me be clear—this kind of situation cannot be repeated. You need to continue showing that you value your team. I believe in second chances, but only when they're earned through consistent action." She paused, studying Mirabel's face. "I'd like to see where you take this next. Leading others isn't just about managing tasks—it's about growing alongside your team, learning from missteps, and becoming better together."

Back in her own office, Mirabel felt her legs go weak as the adrenaline drained away. She sank into her chair, her boss's words echoing in her mind. The fear of losing everything made her hands shake. It wasn't just her job. It was the trust she'd built. She reached for her water bottle.

Mirabel took deep, steadying breaths, willing her racing heart to slow. I could have been fired! After all the work with Maya, it could have ended today. She'd finally begun to understand authentic leadership.

As her breathing steadied, she replayed the interaction with Aisha. I handled myself better than I expected. I didn't cry. I didn't break down. I was truthful. She almost smiled, remembering Aisha's words about noticing the changes in her since Paris. Maybe she was becoming the leader she wanted to be.

The clarity that came with that thought propelled her into action. She called for an immediate team meeting to discuss the product launch that Malik was leading. When everyone gathered, she did something she'd never done before—she started by acknowledging her mistake.

"I need to be honest with all of you," she began, her voice steady despite her nerves. "I haven't always given credit where it was due. I took credit for Rebecca's ideas, and that contributed to her leaving. I want you to know that won't happen again. Each of you deserves recognition for your contributions."

She watched their faces shift from surprise to something that looked like respect. The knot in her stomach began to loosen. Then she turned to Malik. "Could you update us on where we stand with the product launch?"

Malik straightened; his preparation evident as he walked them through his progress. He'd clearly been working behind the scenes, and Mirabel felt a surge of pride—not in herself, but in him.

"Thanks, Malik," she said, meaning it. "I'd like to invite everyone to discuss how we can work together to overcome the remaining obstacles."

To her surprise, ideas started flowing immediately. Each team member spoke up, building on each other's suggestions, their voices carrying a new energy. They weren't just participating—they were engaging. As she sat back and listened, Mirabel realized this was true leadership. It was not about claiming the spotlight but creating space for others to shine.

Once everyone left, Mirabel felt a brief calm. They had clear next steps and a newfound enthusiasm after a tense morning. She'd managed to turn a crisis into something productive—but the cost of getting here still weighed heavily on her conscience.

As Mirabel drove home a whirlwind of emotions stirred within her. She had regained enough composure to get through the day. But the conversation with Aisha echoed in her mind. The weight of her actions pressed down on her, making it difficult to breathe. *I could lose my job over this,* she realized, her hands tightening on the wheel. *How could I have been so shortsighted, so consumed by a scarcity mindset?*

Shame, an old, familiar feeling, rose up from deep within her. *I'm nothing but a fraud, pretending to be nice while only caring about myself.* It took a great deal of self-control not to give in to the self-loathing and blame. Mirabel's mind raced, imagining the potential repercussions of her actions. The fear of losing her job and facing the humiliation was almost too much to bear.

She spiraled even more as she drove. Memories of her career missteps as a leader and manager overwhelmed her. *All those times I put myself first, hurting others while playing the part of the caring boss.* Alone in her car with the weight of regret, she struggled to embrace the self-forgiveness Maya had urged. *How can I possibly forgive myself for this?*

Unable to calm herself, she pulled over, her heart racing. She tried to take deep breaths. Forgiving herself seemed impossible. She needed help. Maya had given her number and said to text if needed. So, she quickly sent a text: *"SOS I'm on the verge of a breakdown and don't know how to cope."*

Maya replied almost immediately, offering to talk by phone in 30 minutes. *"I will try to help,"* Maya texted.

Relief washed over Mirabel, and she regained her composure enough to drive. She found a park where she could walk until Maya's call. She texted Ethan she was running late, and he'd have to do dinner on his own.

She made her way back to her car and called Maya, who picked up after the first ring. "Hello, my dear, what's going on?"

"Maya," her voice quavered, "I almost got fired today. All those things you've been teaching me about living in Scare City? Well, I got caught living right in the middle of it, and I'm terribly embarrassed. All my recent nightmares have came home to roost." Her voice cracked. "I am that person. I am the problem. I wanted to think I didn't live in Scare City but that is exactly where I've been living. I got caught taking credit for a person's contributions on my team. She quit when I was in Paris, but I just found out why and it was my fault." Mirabel took a shuddering breath. "I feel terrible."

Her words tumbled out in a rush; her voice thick with emotion. "It just feels like hell," she finished, her voice barely above a whisper.

Maya listened until Mirabel paused. "I understand where you are right now," she said. "When I practiced law, I had days like you're describing. The constant pressure and feeling trapped in unsolvable situations. Everything seemed to spin out of control, and I couldn't find solid ground. I remember one case in particular..." She hesitated. "Are you in a safe place to close your eyes? Let's go through A.W.A.K.E together."

"Yes," Mirabel said, making sure her car doors were locked, grateful for Maya's availability. She couldn't imagine going home to Ethan in this state.

"Good," Maya said. "Okay. Step 1 is to come into Awareness of your breath. Imagine a cord going from the bottom of your spine all the way down to the center of the Earth. Feel your solid connection to the planet. Breathe."

"Step 2 is to notice your Willingness to be here right now and share what comes to you."

"I want to do this. I want to feel better." Mirabel replied after breathing several times.

"Great," Maya replied. "Appreciation is Step 3, that is to ask yourself, is there anything you can feel grateful about at this moment? And if so, share that with me."

She took a deep breath, then said, "I'm grateful you took my call and that I'm not alone in this. I'm grateful I didn't get fired today. I'm grateful that I handled the situation as well as I did."

"Beautiful," Maya encouraged. "Now we move into Step 4, which is Kindness. This is a little different. I want you to kindly tune into your younger self and see what's happening for her right now."

Mirabel's thoughts drifted to her younger self when she felt inadequate. She recalled the sensation of being utterly lost, her mind racing with chaotic uncertainty. Her voice wavered as she described these memories. Her past struggles weighing on every word, but eventually a wave of kindness and compassion flooded into her awareness.

"I can feel a sense of love flowing through me," she said smiling with her eyes still closed.

"Okay, good," Maya said. "Now for the final step, Embodiment: I want you to see yourself embracing that younger version of you. I invite you to shower her with the approval and reassurance she has always craved. Share with her that she is enough, that she is whole and complete, and see what else comes up."

As tears rolled down her face, Mirabel spoke to her younger self: "*You have all that you need. You are limitless. You're going to be okay. I love you so much.*"

Maya continued, "Notice if you want to offer forgiveness to yourself or anyone else."

"Yes, I want to forgive myself, but it isn't easy."

"Okay, stay with that feeling and see what happens."

"Focus on your breathing," Maya guided Mirabel. "Let go of it with each exhalation. Allow this process of forgiving yourself."

Mirabel followed Maya's words and eventually her own inner voice took over. It began guiding her to inhale love and exhale the past along with her mistakes. As calmness washed over her, Maya continued, "Allow yourself to feel peace in this moment. Be here now."

In the quiet, Mirabel had an epiphany. "I see now," she shared, "my success is linked to my team's. True leadership is about fostering others' growth, not just my personal success."

"That's beautiful," Maya responded, and stopping talking to give her time to process.

"I want to share something transformative with you. A mentor once taught me to view every obstacle as a hidden opportunity. Within each hardship lies potential for growth that often surpasses the difficulty itself."

Her voice softened with conviction. "But here's the key: you must first identify what's really holding you back. Once you recognize that internal barrier, you can begin dismantling it. Only then can you access the unexpected gifts concealed within your struggles."

Mirabel leaned back in the driver's seat, letting Maya's words sink in through the phone speaker. Her grip on the steering wheel loosened as she spoke. "That really resonates with me," she said thoughtfully. "I think my biggest barrier has been fear – fear of not being enough, of letting people down. But maybe..." she paused, watching a leaf drift past her windshield, "maybe that fear isn't protecting me at all. It's just keeping me from taking the risks that could help everyone grow."

She adjusted her phone. "When you talk about hidden opportunities, I can see now how my struggles with delegation weren't just about control. They were chances to build trust, to let others shine. I was so focused on avoiding failure that I couldn't see the potential for collective success."

Maya spoke, "I'm glad this is making more sense to you now. With all you've been through recently, I believe you're fully embracing the Fourth Catalyst. Soon you'll enter into the Fifth Catalyst—Define Your Own Abundance, but I'll let that unfold naturally."

Mirabel thanked her. As they ended their call, a sense of calm settled over her. Pulling into her driveway, she hesitated. Ethan was probably wondering where she'd been. *How much should she share? How much could he understand?* With a sigh, she stepped out of the car. Whatever came next, she knew this conversation wouldn't be easy.

Mirabel found Ethan at his desk, staring out at the trees in the fading dusk light.

"Hi," she said with uncertainty as she stood leaning against the doorway, making an effort to be present. "You seem deep in thought. What's going on?"

Ethan smiled; his eyes still focused on the view. "We landed a great new client. They're paying more than double what our old client was paying."

Mirabel's eyes widened. "That's wonderful! I know it wasn't easy letting go of that toxic client. I'm proud of you for making that tough call."

"Thanks," Ethan said, as he turned his attention to Mirabel. "Even the little I've learned about what Maya is teaching you is helping me. It's still a work in progress. But I'm looking at my business in new ways and I'm excited about what's happening. It's how I want my work to be."

Mirabel nodded. "I am happy for you. Congratulations! We're both learning as we go. Sometimes I wish I was further along, and I give myself a hard time for not seeing things sooner. But then I remind myself that it's okay to be where I am right now. It takes time to change." She paused, her expression shifting. "And speaking of journeys, something tough happened today at work. I managed it well, all things considered, but it was a rough day."

He looked at her with genuine concern. "What happened?"

She took a deep breath, her gaze lowering. "I... I did something I'm not proud of," she began. "Remember Rebecca from my team? The one who quit while I was in Paris?" She twisted her wedding ring. "She left because of me. I took credit for her ideas, made them seem like my own. Aisha found out today."

Her voice grew quieter. "I could have lost my job, Ethan. I think I almost did. But more than that... I'm realizing how much I've hurt people by acting this way. It wasn't just Rebecca. I've done this before, always trying to prove myself, always afraid of not measuring up." She looked up at him finally, her eyes glistening. "Aisha gave me another chance, but God, I feel so ashamed of who I've been."

The words felt different now after her talk with Maya. They were still painful, but clearer. Naming her actions to her husband made both their weight and her path forward more real.

Tears welled in Mirabel's eyes as she continued, her voice trembling with emotion. Ethan leaned in listening intently as she opened up about her actions, her regrets, and the fears and insecurities that had driven her behavior.

Moved by her vulnerability, he stood and walked to Mirabel wrapping his arms around her in a comforting embrace. After a month of distance, she allowed herself to relax into his warmth, finding solace in his presence. He rubbed her back gently and placed a soft kiss on her forehead.

After a moment of silence, he spoke softly, "I'm so sorry you're going through this. And I apologize for how things have been between us. I haven't been making it any easier, have I?"

His words seemed to break a dam within Mirabel. Her tears began to flow freely as she released the pent-up tension she'd been holding onto. In the safety of Ethan's embrace, she found the courage to express her feelings.

"No, you haven't made this easier," she admitted, quiet but firm. "You've been really tough on me. You may not like hearing it, but our old thinking trapped us in stress and conflict. We were always berating ourselves. That's not living." She took a shaky breath. "I can't go backwards. I'm lucky I still have my job after what happened today, and I know I have to change. You have to change too."

He nodded, his shoulders relaxing slightly. "I hear you. I know I've been messing up lately. I want you to be honest with me. How can I help you?"

She stepped back from his embrace and met his gaze. This was the moment Maya said would come—when he was truly ready to listen. She drew in a steadying breath.

"Ethan, I've been working with Maya to understand our differences better. While I appreciate your desire to help us build wealth, when you dictate what I can and cannot do, it makes me feel diminished." Her voice wavered slightly but grew stronger. "I know you don't intend to treat me like a child, but that's how it feels when you talk to me that way. It might seem minor to you, but this pattern keeps repeating, and addressing it would show me you truly care. Can we find a way to move past this?"

He considered her words carefully, his usual quick responses held in check. "I apologize. I hadn't realized how my comments were affecting you. You're right—I dismissed it as unimportant. I thought I was helping us stay on track. What do you need me to do differently?"

She inhaled deeply. "I need you to trust me and my decisions," she began, her voice steady despite the emotion behind it. "I'm just beginning to understand that many things I thought I wanted were attempts to fill the void left when my father moved out. He was my anchor, my safety in the world, and then suddenly he was gone." Tears traced silent paths down her cheeks. "Since then, I've tried to fill that emptiness with money and silence and perfectionism, and now I see how these behaviors have been suffocating me. I need to be able to express myself without it spiraling into an argument, for starters."

His eyes widened with understanding. "Okay, I hear you. I had no idea... Fighting with you is the last thing I want. I'm so sorry."

"And I need room to try new things," she continued, "even if I stumble sometimes. Making mistakes is how we learn, and I'm ready to embrace that." She met his gaze with raw honesty. "I want to learn better money management while still finding joy in life. I don't want to feel weighed down or bitter about our finances. Can we find a middle ground that allows for both responsibility and fulfillment?"

His gaze drifted over her shoulder before returning to hers. She saw him wrestling with his response, his pragmatism yielding to deeper emotions.

"I never meant to diminish you or seem dismissive," he said, vulnerability threading through his voice. "I want to be present for you. Truly present." He swallowed hard. "Since this started with your trip, I've been examining my own fears and how they've shaped my actions. My parents were constantly struggling financially, and I was terrified of repeating their pattern. So I went to the opposite extreme. But in doing so, I've been holding us back from really living."

She wrapped her arms around herself, processing his words. "I appreciate you saying that," she said carefully. "But I don't expect things to change overnight. What I need is for you to learn how to pause and really think about things from my perspective." She brushed at her tears with the back of her hand. "And I know I need to work on this too. I haven't always been good at telling you how I feel until I'm already overwhelmed. Maybe we both need to practice slowing down, checking in with each other before things get too hard."

She met his eyes again, her expression both tender and guarded. "This conversation is important, but it's just the beginning. We both have patterns to unlearn."

He nodded slowly, and she could see him fighting the urge to jump to solutions. "You're right," he said finally. "We've got a lot of work ahead of us. But I'm here for it. For all of it."

They embraced once more and kissed. She felt a sense of love and support she'd been craving for a very long time. She recognized their shared humanity—the inevitability of mistakes, the necessity of growth. In that moment, her appreciation for herself and Ethan deepened. Every challenge was not just an obstacle, but a lesson in resilience.

Walking to the kitchen, peace washed over Mirabel and a realization dawned: she really could face any challenge, personal or professional. This newfound confidence wrapped her like a protective cloak, making her feel safer in her own skin.

Define Your Own Abundance

"Abundance flows not from an overflowing bank account,
but from an overflowing heart."
~Brené Brown

The morning sun bathed Ocean Beach in golden light as Mirabel and Tanya walked along the water's edge during their monthly ritual. Salt spray kissed their faces while waves crashed against the shore.

Mirabel turned to her friend, her expression softening with the relief of sharing with someone who truly understood. "I want to update you on what's been happening with Ethan and I," she began.

"For weeks, I'd been sleeping on the couch," Mirabel explained, her voice softening. "At first, we couldn't find any middle ground. But for the first time in years, I stood my ground."

Tanya listened attentively, nodding as Mirabel continued.

"I needed space to heal, to find my voice again," Mirabel said. "Ironically, that distance created an opening for us to reconnect." Her tone growing more serious. "Then I almost lost my job which I texted you about. All said, I was forced to confront some choices I'm not proud of."

Mirabel's voice strengthened as she went on. "Finally, I opened up to Ethan about everything that wasn't working between us. The whole truth."

Her eyes brightened. "It was like flipping a switch. Suddenly, we were really communicating—talking and listening."

A warm smile spread across Mirabel's face. "It's only been a few days, but the change is remarkable. I'm back in our bed, and Ethan's making a real effort to be more loving and supportive. We're both working on our communication. It feels like a fresh start."

Tanya reached out, squeezing Mirabel's hand supportively. "I'm so proud of you for standing up for yourself and your relationship," she said. "That takes real courage."

She returned the squeeze, feeling anchored by her friend's support. "Thank you. It hasn't been easy, but I know it was necessary."

"So, how are things at work now?" Tanya asked, her voice gentle with concern.

"Better than I expected, actually. I'm implementing some changes in my leadership approach." She paused, considering her words. "We have our project reveal to the executive team in a few weeks, and I think these changes will make a real difference."

"That's great to hear," Tanya encouraged. "What kind of changes?"

"Well, I'm focusing more on being present for my team," she explained with newfound enthusiasm. "I'm really trying to understand their needs and how I can help them achieve their goals alongside the company's. It's been... eye-opening."

Tanya nodded; her interest piqued. "It sounds like you're embracing a more collaborative approach. That must be quite a shift."

"It is," Mirabel agreed. She turned to Tanya, her expression genuinely curious. "You know, all these changes have got me thinking. I'm remembering our conversation last month, and I know you manage people too."

She paused briefly, the gentle waves providing a soothing backdrop. "I was wondering... Have you had any new insights? About this idea of being and having enough? In your work or personal life?" Mirabel smiled warmly at her friend. "If so, I'd love to hear about them."

Tanya looked out to the sea. "You know, it's interesting you ask," she began slowly. "Since our last conversation, I've been doing a lot of reflecting on what something like abundance and scarcity really means to me. And that information you sent me from your coach really hit home."

She continued as they resumed their walk. "I've come to see how it goes far beyond money. It's about faith, courage, and community too. These elements have been guiding me through some challenges and decisions lately at work."

Mirabel nodded encouragingly, prompting Tanya to elaborate.

"I've been thinking," Tanya explained, "that staying true to my values isn't just about me or my family or the nonprofit. It's about contributing to the broader community too." She sighed. "I think we often miss the bigger picture when it comes to having enough or being enough."

Her pace slowed as she continued, "It's not just about material things. It's about feeling fulfilled, feeling like you matter. Like what you do makes a difference." She turned to Mirabel, her eyes bright with conviction. "I guess what I'm saying is that I am seeing this topic in a whole new light."

Tanya's animated features became more contemplative. "There's something else I've been considering. For many people, especially in marginalized communities, lack and scarcity isn't just a mindset. It's rooted in historical and systemic issues."

Mirabel drew closer to hear her over the waves. Her face softened with interest. She studied her friend's profile against the gray-blue horizon. Tanya's usual easy smile had given way to a more serious look.

"We see it in challenges to voting rights, justice system inequalities, and health disparities. Even well-resourced women of color face these issues. It's like... scarcity manifests as limited access to basic rights."

She took a breath before adding, "In a way, the scarcity we're really struggling with is a scarcity of compassion, honesty, and courage to do the right thing. It's the inability to see all people as equal."

Mirabel was quiet, letting Tanya's words sink in. Finally, she responded, "I think I understand what you're saying. We can't ignore the hard stuff, but we can choose how we respond to it."

She then added, "Maybe it's about finding a balance. Acknowledging the challenges, and focusing on what we can change?"

Tanya's face brightened as she spoke, "YES! When one of us does better, it lifts all of us up."

"What I'm learning is helping me see life in a bigger way," Mirabel said, growing animated. "I'm noticing where my habits come from, whether they serve me. Learning self-compassion is changing how I think."

She dug her toes into the sand. "I feel like others could benefit from this kind of self-reflection. It might help them understand people different from themselves better. That's what's happening for me, at least."

"Yeah, I get that," Tanya said, her eyes meeting Mirabel's. "It's amazing how changing the way we think, even a little bit, can make such a big difference in our lives and how we relate to others."

The two friends headed back to their cars in comfortable silence, letting the conversation sink in. They both knew that changing ingrained habits and thoughts wasn't easy, but they also saw the value in having these discussions.

"I'm glad you're finding something that resonates with you," Tanya said. "It would be wonderful if this helps you find new ways to bring people together."

Her gaze drifting to the horizon. "You know what I mean? Far too often people focus only on themselves instead of their community, or they're always rushing around without really connecting with people. It can make the world feel like a very lonely place sometimes, even when we're surrounded by people."

Mirabel felt chills run up and down her body in response to what Tanya was saying. "I get it. I don't want to do this just for myself. I want to find a way to make things better for everyone, you know?"

Tanya smiled, giving Mirabel's shoulder a gentle squeeze. "That's a big goal, but it's a good one. Can't wait to see where this takes you."

At Mirabel's car, emotion swelled within her chest. "Thanks for listening," she murmured, drawing Tanya into an embrace that conveyed what words couldn't. "Your support means everything."

Tanya's expression shifted into a mix of amusement and exasperation. "Speaking of support," she said, "what about the fundraiser? You know, the one you seem to miss every year?" She raised an eyebrow. "Did you talk to Ethan about coming this time?"

Mirabel's face fell. "Oh no," she groaned. "With everything going on, it completely slipped my mind. I'm so sorry. I'll talk to Ethan tonight and let you know, I promise."

"You better!" she replied, both playful and sincere. "I'm counting on you. This event means a lot to me, and I'd love to have you there."

Mirabel nodded. "I understand. I'll do my best to make it happen."

Mirabel buckled up and started the car, then paused. The weight of their conversation washed over her, Tanya's words echoing in her mind and sparking new perspectives. How might these ideas help to shape her path forward?

Pulling out of the parking lot, she felt both excitement and curiosity wash over her. As she tapped the touchscreen, Taylor Swift's "Begin Again" flowed through the car's speakers. The song painted a picture of someone finding unexpected joy in a new beginning, a perfect match for her state of mind. The song's hopeful melody accompanied her thoughts, turning the familiar drive home into a journey of new possibilities.

A foggy morning found Mirabel at her kitchen table, journal open beside her coffee. The pages traced her transformation: her Paris flight where she'd written her deepest wishes, her moments of feeling lost, reaching out to Lawrence.

Each entry revealed another layer—the Catalysts that had guided her, the dreams that whispered truths, the reflections after meditation. Through talks with Ethan, Tanya, and Aisha a pattern emerged. Her father's abandonment had shaped everything—driving her to constantly prove her worth, to fill an impossible void.

That early loss had taught her that safety was fragile, that loved ones could vanish. She'd responded by building walls of caution and hard work, mistaking security for freedom.

But since that time with Leila in Paris, so much has been shifting. Mirabel was discovering a different kind of abundance—one that flowed from within, from living authentically rather than gathering more.

Looking at how far she'd come, she felt a surge of gratitude. She wondered if Leila knew the impact she'd had, how her gentle observations had set these changes in motion. Mirabel grabbed her phone to share her insights with the woman who had first helped her.

"Leila! How are you? How is Stu doing?" Mirabel asked when Leila answered her phone.

"We're good," Leila replied. "Actually, we've been building a garden in our backyard. It's been amazing—working with my hands, getting inspiration from nature. What about you?"

"That sounds wonderful," Mirabel said, genuinely intrigued. "I might need to pick your brain about gardening soon. As for me, I've been continuing to work with the coach I told you about. I'm cultivating greater self-trust and it's transforming parts of my life I didn't even realizing needed changing."

"Wow, that's fantastic!" Leila exclaimed. "What's that been like for you?"

"It's... liberating. It's like I've been carrying an invisible weight for years without knowing it. Now when I make decisions, there's this quiet certainty beneath them. And it feels really good to trust myself."

Eager to learn from her friend's wisdom, Mirabel shifted the focus. "You know, Leila, you seem to embody abundance effortlessly. You radiate such positivity. What's your secret to staying so present and content?"

Leila paused for a moment, then shared her perspective. "Hmmmm, that's a great question. Let's see... Most people identify with the things in life that will fade—our beauty, possessions, personality, and even beliefs. They are all momentary appearances in life itself. Yet what stands the test of time, what really matters, is the formless energy from which all things emerge. When I am able to identify with this is when I feel my best. I feel connected to everyone and everything without being sucked into the drama of life. That's when joy becomes sustainable for me."

Mirabel was impressed. "I think I'm learning this, but I have a long way to go before I could live that way all the time. You inspire me."

"Ethan and I are working through it together. It was rough at first, but he's come around. He's even reviewing the worksheets and practices she's teaching me!"

Leila's voice brightened. "That sounds awesome!"

She smiled. "From talking with you and Tanya, I'm seeing how abundance looks different for everyone. We each find our own path."

"I see," Leila replied. "It changes how we look at life. And it is very personal."

"Yes, for sure!" Mirabel's eyes lit up.

Mirabel pressed her hand to her heart, feeling the warmth of her connection with Leila. "Thank you for sharing your perspective. You always give me more to think about."

After the call, she got up, made a cup of tea, and went out to the patio. In the quiet of the morning, her thoughts drifted to Ethan. A wave of longing washed over her as she realized how much she missed spending quality time with her husband. Her own self-discovery and their new talks sparked a wish to reconnect more with him.

As she sat there on her patio, a memory from earlier that week surfaced, bringing a smile to her face. She had approached Ethan about Tanya's nonprofit fundraiser, an event he typically avoided.

"Oh, and before I forget," she had said, her voice tentative but hopeful, "Tanya wants us to go to her nonprofit's annual fundraiser this year. I know you don't like those events, but this is important, and I want to support her efforts. Are you okay with that?"

He had hesitated for a moment, and Mirabel had braced herself for the usual polite refusal. But to her surprise, he nodded. "Sure, let's go to the gala. Let her know we're coming."

A sense of joy washed over her. "Thanks for working with me on this," she had replied with barely contained excitement. "It will be fun, and you don't have to worry about me buying stuff at the silent auction. I promise!"

She had texted Tanya with the good news, her heart light with the prospect of not only supporting her friend but also sharing this experience with Ethan. It was a small step, but it felt like a significant one.

She thought of Ethan and their recent progress. How can we continue to nurture this renewed connection, she wondered, and gradually strengthen our relationship?

She sipped her tea, considering simple steps they could take: maybe scheduling a weekly date night, or setting aside time each evening to really talk about their day. Nothing grandiose, just small, consistent efforts to stay connected. As a gentle breeze rustled the plants outside, Mirabel felt a sense of hope.

Mirabel's phone buzzed and she blinked at the unexpected text from their friend Bin: *"You two should use the cabin this weekend. It's about time. Keys under the mat."*

She read it again, confused. In the three years since Bin had bought the mountain getaway, he'd never once offered it to them. He knew about Ethan's careful budgeting—how casual mentions of weekend trips would trigger detailed cost calculations including gas, groceries, and car wear and tear. *Why was he suddenly being so generous?*

Mirabel stepped into their bedroom where Ethan was reading, her heart fluttering with nervous hope. "Look at this," she said, holding out her phone.

Ethan glanced up from his book. She watched his face as he read the message, waiting for the familiar furrow of his brow, the start of practical objections. Instead, he looked up at her with an unexpected grin.

"We could leave after lunch tomorrow," he said. "Beat the traffic."

"What?" Mirabel blinked. "You mean... you want to go?"

"I'll move my afternoon meetings to next week." He was already reaching for his laptop. "Want to make a packing list?"

Hours later, lying in bed, Mirabel mapped their impromptu getaway. She marveled at the strangeness of it all—not just Bin's unprecedented offer, but Ethan's immediate yes. Something had shifted in both of them, and she couldn't wait to see where it might lead.

As they drove across the Bay Bridge, Mirabel watched Ethan's profile in the afternoon sun. The weight of what she needed to say pressed at her chest. But Maya's coaching had taught her the value of vulnerability.

"Ethan," she began. "When we first met, I was a financial wreck," she admitted. "The student loans, the credit cards—I had no plan for any of it. I never thanked you for helping me out of that hole. I know I've been avoiding learning about our finances since then."

Something in his expression shifted, a tension she hadn't realized he carried seeming to ease. "I worried constantly," he confessed. "If anything happened to me, you wouldn't know where to start. And honestly? Being the only one responsible for our financial security—it's been lonely."

She reached for his hand. "I'm ready to be an equal partner in this. Maya has helped me realize how I've dodged responsibility for my thoughts and actions. Last week, I actually acknowledged when my team's approach was better than mine and let them take the lead." Her eyes softened. "Owning my choices instead of defending them feels... empowering. Change is possible."

"I'm sorry for being controlling about the money," he said, his voice carrying a new vulnerability. "I'm working on it. You said what we focus on expands—maybe it's time we focus on growing together."

From then on, the drive flew by, filled with conversation, newfound closeness, and spontaneous stops at roadside stands where Mirabel couldn't resist getting food for their meals. At the cabin, they unpacked and cooked dinner together. Over the meal, they discussed future plans, including the possibility of having children—a once distant idea that felt more possible now. They considered how parenthood would shift their priorities beyond work and money.

The next morning, they woke early for a hike. The trails were muddy from melting snow but still manageable. Mirabel couldn't help but notice Ethan's athletic prowess. He bounded ahead, leaving her to navigate the squishy terrain at her own pace. She felt a familiar twinge of self-doubt and her mind began to wander to the past. She remembered how she'd always struggled to keep up in physical activities and the people who had given her a hard time about it. She could hear their comments in her head, making her feel small and inadequate.

But then, Maya's words cut through. *You have no reason to judge yourself. The past is gone, and you're not any of it. You live in the present, always becoming your future.* It was like a lightbulb went off in her mind. She realized she had been dragging around so many old insecurities. She'd let them define her, even though they had no impact now. She was not the same person as before and could choose her own thoughts.

She saw how she'd been her own harshest critic. As she learned to quiet her negative internal voice, she became kinder overall. By refraining from judgment, complaints, and gossip, she attracted more positivity. She recognized that her changed intention was influencing the attitudes of those around her.

As she took in the beauty of the forest, she felt grateful to be out in nature and for her body's ability to move, no matter the speed. The present moment was what mattered. With each squishy step along the trail, she felt a new sense of self-acceptance.

As Ethan came back into view, she smiled. "Normally when you race ahead, I get so frustrated," she admitted. "But today, it was perfect. The solo time in this gorgeous setting helped me process some realizations."

She reached for his hand, intertwining their fingers. "I'm learning how to let go and to trust in the journey. And there's no one I'd rather be on this wild, wonderful path with than you. I love you."

He pulled her close, his eyes sparkling with love. "Well, I'm thrilled to have you back by my side. I love you. And hey, if you ever need another head start, let me know. I'm happy to play the role of the speedy hare to your wise, introspective tortoise."

She swatted his arm. "Watch it, mister. This tortoise might surprise you one of these days."

Their laughter echoed through the trees as they hiked on and returned to the cabin late in the afternoon. Mirabel had secretly planned a special surprise. She asked him to start a fire and put on music. She prepared a six-course Mexican-inspired feast using ingredients from the roadside stands they stopped at on their drive. The kind of meal her paternal grandmother used to make when she was a child. She had died of cancer when Mirabel was seven but her love of Mexican food never faded.

Together they put the dishes on the table. Fresh chips with mango habanero salsa, guacamole, and queso. Each dish she unveiled was a work of art. She'd bought fresh shrimp ceviche. It had lively citrus notes. She warmed the velvety corn and hatch chili chowder. Then steamed the savory chicken tamales and fried the carne asada for tacos. They savored each bite, losing themselves in the sensory experience.

"I haven't had Mexican food this good since my family trips to Baja as a kid," he said. "Thank you for putting so much thought into this."

She wanted him to feel as pampered as she did in Paris, appreciating the moment fully. After enjoying key lime cheesecake flan for dessert, they settled into an evening of affection and intimacy in the cozy cabin feeling gratitude for the wonderful day together and for each other.

"Oh, and I have a surprise for you too!" he announced with a playful glint in his eye.

"I've been brushing up on my massage skills. Ready to be spoiled?"

She grinned ear to ear. "Do you even have to ask?"

He led her to the bedroom, where he had prepared a comfy massage setup. As she settled in, he began to work his magic, kneading away the knots and tension from her body.

"Mmm, this feels amazing," she murmured, her eyes fluttering closed. "Where did you learn these skills?"

He chuckled. "YouTube. I wanted to surprise you."

As his hands worked, they fell into a comfortable silence, broken only by the mellow strains of Joan Armatrading's "Love and Affection" drifting through the room. The song's soulful guitar and rich vocals wove around them, creating a memorable connection. His fingers moved with ease, deliberate yet tender. The warmth of his touch and the familiar scent of his skin enveloped her, drawing her deeper into the moment.

When he finished, Ethan's hands stilled on Mirabel's back. She felt the mattress shift as he leaned closer, his breath warm against her skin. Slowly, she turned to face him, meeting his gaze. His eyes, dark and full of unspoken emotion, held hers.

With gentle movements, he drew her close. His strong arms encircled her, the soft cotton of his T-shirt brushing against her bare shoulders. She nestled into his embrace, her body still relaxed from the massage, fitting perfectly against the contours of his chest.

"I love you so much," he whispered, his voice thick with emotion. "I am so lucky to have you in my life."

She tilted her head up, her eyes shining. "I love you too. You make me feel safe, cherished... and so incredibly loved."

In that instant, as the last notes of a sultry song faded, she felt a strong sense of belonging in his arms. It filled her heart with quiet joy. Their closeness—skin touching, the scent of oil, his soft touch—was more than just physical. For the first time, she surrendered completely to the present, embracing the beautiful certainty that in his arms, she had found her home.

Slowly, she leaned in, her lips meeting his. As the kiss deepened, the world around them seemed to fade away, leaving only the two of them, lost in their own private universe of love and passion.

The next morning, they lounged in bed, snuggling and lovingly looking into each other's eyes. Mirabel felt a surge of thoughts she wanted to express. Ethan, still groggy, was content in their shared warmth.

"Ethan," Mirabel said brightly, "can I share something?"

"Of course," he mumbled, blinking slowly but giving her his full attention.

She smiled contemplatively as she reflected on their love and the weekend's revelations.

"I used to think it would take some earth-shattering realization," she mused, tracing patterns on his arm. "But now I see that abundance is within everyone's reach. It's a matter of focusing on what brings us joy and letting go of the negativity that holds us back."

He nodded, becoming more alert as he listened.

She continued, "I've also learned that life isn't passive. We can't sit back and wait for good things to happen to us. It's an active journey where we have the capacity to shape our own destinies and become the people we want to be."

He smiled, now fully awake. "Sounds like a plan to me," he said, pulling her closer.

Basking in their renewed lovingness, they embraced the morning's simple joys. A crackling fire chased away the chill as they prepared a hearty breakfast together. Later, they went outside and laughed like children as they rolled the wet spring snow into a lopsided snowman.

As they packed to leave, they chatted. They recalled funny moments and discussed potential dates for their next trip. The cabin had served its purpose well, offering them a much-needed break from routine and a chance to reconnect.

"I can't wait to explore the coast near Benbow," she said after they'd started on their drive back home. Her eyes sparkled with anticipation. "People say the rugged cliffs and beaches there are breathtaking."

"And Yosemite would be amazing," he added, his voice filled with excitement. "I've seen so many stunning photos of the valley on Instagram recently, and I can't wait to experience its beauty in person."

Her face lit up. "Oh, Yosemite! I've dreamed of staying at the Ahwahnee Hotel since I was a little girl. I remember when my dad first took us camping there, and we walked around the grand hotel one day. It was like stepping into a fairy tale. The hotel is expensive. But it's a magical place full of history and surrounded by the park's natural beauty. Staying there would be a dream come true."

With an hour left of their drive home, Mirabel's phone buzzed from her bag on the floor. Seeing her mother's name on the screen made her stomach clench. She and Sheena hadn't spoken in weeks—not since before her Paris trip. Mirabel's relaxed, post-weekend mood evaporating as she contemplated letting it go to voicemail.

Better to face it now. "Hi, mom."

"Honey, I didn't want to bother you," Sheena's voice was shaking. "I'm in a desperate state. I thought I had a handle on things, but I just can't..." She dissolved into tears.

"Mom," Mirabel said, all too familiar with this conversation—they'd had it at least five times in the last year alone. "Don't cry. I'll call you when I'm home tonight. We can figure this out."

"Okay," Sheena sniffled. "I'll be waiting for your call."

After hanging up, Mirabel's heart sank. Her mother's financial troubles had caused more tension between her and Ethan than she cared to admit. She turned to him, noting his white-knuckled grip on the steering wheel. "I'm conflicted. I want to help, but I know we can't keep rescuing her."

He sighed. "We need to be careful and proceed with caution."

A silence fell between them. She gazed out the window, her mind drifting to her childhood. After a while, she broke the quiet with a soft admission.

"You know," she began, "I've been thinking about my mom throughout this process. About how her constant money struggles affected me growing up." She took a breath. "I realized how—because of her—I never learned to see money as a tool. Instead, it became this... looming threat. I guess you could say I learned to fear money rather than understand it."

He squeezed her hand. "I know we've given her money in the past, but what if we brainstorm some ideas to support her rather than fixing the problem for her? We can help her with a budget, find a counselor—that kind of thing."

"Those are good ideas," she said.

"We need to set boundaries," he advised. "Guiding and supporting is good, but your mom must take responsibility."

She agreed, seeing in this challenge another opportunity for healing. As they pulled into their driveway, she felt apprehensive about what lay ahead but ready to apply Maya's teachings.

"Our journey just got more interesting," she said with a grimace.

He squeezed her leg. "We've got this, babe. I love you so much. Together, we can handle anything."

The following Saturday, Mirabel and Ethan prepared for their dinner party. They had invited their closest friends for a celebration, but with a twist—one their guests weren't yet aware of. As they worked, arranging flowers and candles around their home, they exchanged knowing glances.

"They might be surprised," Ethan said, adding plates to the table, "but I'm sure they'll be up for it. Our friends are pretty adventurous."

The guest list included an eclectic mix: Leila and her boyfriend Stu; Tanya; Bin and his wife Shelly; and David with his husband John. Mirabel had put a cryptic note in each invitation, hinting at special questions they'd ask after dinner. It had undoubtedly piqued their friends' curiosity.

The house was filled with delicious aromas teasing a lovely meal to come. Mirabel's famous chicken and spinach stew simmered on the stove—sure to be a hit with their friends.

With the final touches in place—flowers arranged, candles lit, and table set—Mirabel and Ethan took a moment to appreciate the warm, inviting atmosphere they'd created that was perfect for the evening ahead.

"Everything looks amazing," Ethan said, wrapping an arm around Mirabel's waist. "Are you ready for this?"

Mirabel leaned into him, nodding. "More than ready. I'm excited to share our journey and see where it leads our friends."

As guests arrived, the feast grew more impressive. Bin brought colorful fried rice teeming with vegetables. John and David arrived with an array of cheeses, crackers, and unique dips. Leila's crisp vegetable salad added a fresh touch, while Tanya contributed a spread of vegetarian dips and salads. For dessert, chocolate-dipped strawberries and a decadent flourless chocolate cake awaited.

They gathered around the table clinking glasses. They toasted to good company and great food. Conversation flowed easily, punctuated by laughter and stories. Leila and Mirabel regaled everyone with tales from Paris, while others chimed in with their own travel anecdotes.

As the last bites of dessert were savored, Mirabel ushered everyone into the living room, where they settled into a tight huddle. She could see the curiosity on each of their faces.

Mirabel exchanged a warm glance with Ethan before breaking into a smile. "Ever since I came back from Paris, Ethan and I have been on this enlightening journey." She paused, gathering her thoughts. "It started with me hiring someone – I call her my Catalyst coach – but it's grown into something much deeper. We've been discovering ways to live more richly, more fully."

Leaning forward with an infectious energy, her eyes sparkling, she continued, "We thought we'd try something special tonight. Would you share a moment when you felt truly abundant? It doesn't have to be about money – just any time you felt completely overflowing with joy, or love, or wonder... any kind of goodness?"

"And don't worry," Ethan added with a grin, "we'll go first."

Leila's eyes lit up. "Oh, I love this idea! It's like we're all sharing secret recipes for happiness."

Mirabel nodded, smiling. "Exactly! We're on a treasure hunt for the richest moments in our lives."

Ethan added, "These treasures don't have to cost much. They're experiences that made us feel alive and grateful."

"Let's get started," Mirabel said, clapping her hands.

Mirabel began to share about the time at the Louvre with Leila. Leila chimed in with a few details. Mirabel acted out the art historian's dramatic gestures and made everyone laugh. "It was like stepping into a painting and becoming part of the art!" she exclaimed. "And the best part? It didn't cost all that much!"

Ethan went next, sharing his unforgettable experience at Tough Mudder. "Imagine swimming through a giant chocolate pudding, but instead of pudding, it's mud!" he said, grinning. "I felt like a kid, playing in the dirt and pushing myself to the limit. Sure, I needed stitches at the end of the day, but it was worth every bit of the pain."

As each friend took their turn, the room filled with laughter, gasps, and nods of understanding. Leila's story of finding a place to rent in New York City thanks to a kind stranger left everyone in awe. "It was like the city itself was looking out for me," she said. "And the best part? I could actually afford the rent!"

John shared his story of falling gravely ill in Bali. His harrowing experience revealed the true nature of his friends and how much they'd helped him get through it. A nightmare became a lesson about the value of genuine connections.

Bin shared his experience. He got an unexpected inheritance from his uncle. It changed his life. David recounted his European backpacking adventure. He made priceless friendships along the way. Shelly's story of finding her passion and love through a life-altering college job inspired everyone.

Tanya went next. She shared, "I felt abundant at my college commencement when I received the honor of *magna cum laude*. No one in my family had gone to college before, and there I was, graduating with the highest honors. My family was so proud of me. I was so proud of myself. Breaking through all those barriers brought me tremendous feelings of abundance."

"Gosh, I'll never forget that day. You were and are a superstar. I am so proud of you," Mirabel replied.

Stu went next, looking at Leila with warmth. His cheeks flushed as he recounted spotting her at the farmers market, both reaching for the last bunch of sunflowers. "She insisted I take them," he said, squeezing her hand. "But I gave her half the bunch instead. Those flowers lasted a week, but here we are two years later. Sometimes abundance comes from being willing to share what little you have."

Mirabel felt a deep gratitude wash over her as she listened. Each story spoke to how happiness grew from connection and care. "It's remarkable," she observed softly, "how generosity seems to multiply itself when we stay open to it."

As the evening wound down, friends lingered in small groups. They hugged Mirabel and Ethan at the door, several mentioning plans to host their own abundance parties. "Who knew a simple dinner party could spark so much?" Leila said to Mirabel.

After the last guest left, Mirabel and Ethan moved through their living room in comfortable silence gathering plates. Ethan paused, still holding an empty wine glass. "You know what struck me?" he said finally. "Every story tonight was really about transformation—how people found richness in places they weren't even looking for it. Hearing everyone's stories got me thinking."

She looked up from the plate she was washing and smiled. "Oh? What's on your mind?"

He leaned against the kitchen counter; his brow furrowed. "I am seeing how what you said was right. In my pursuit of money, I lost sight of the things that make me feel alive. That spark had faded, and I didn't even notice until now."

She walked over to give him a big hug. "I hear you. Our lives before this were all about work. We'd forgotten how to enjoy the moments that matter."

He nodded, his eyes meeting hers. "Hearing John's story about traveling in Bali. And David's tale of the friendships he made while backpacking. All of the stories actually, they made me see how much I've been missing. You were right. We need to change."

"So, what do you want to do?" she asked, her eyes sparkling.

He thought for a moment before answering. "I want to start by focusing on the things that make me feel alive. Like tonight, I shared my Tough Mudder experience. I remembered how alive I felt pushing myself to the limit. I found out what I was capable of."

He grinned. "I'm thinking about training for a marathon or triathlon in Marin this fall. I know it's a long shot, but I want to get back into shape and challenge myself like I used to. Those were the times when I felt the most powerful, the most fulfilled."

Her face lit up. "That's an incredible goal! I'll support you every step of the way."

He pulled her into a tight embrace, his heart swelling with gratitude. "I love you. Thank you for pushing me, even when I resisted. I can see how this is what we both needed."

He leaned in and kissed her, pouring all of his love into the gesture. When they parted, Mirabel's eyes were shining.

She smiled, "I'm excited to see where this takes us. I'm thinking about pulling out my watercolors again. I can feel my creativity rekindling. I know we can find the magic that we've been missing. It's so funny because Maya said we would be figuring out what abundance meant to each of us. I think that became fully apparent tonight."

As they got ready for bed, she could sense a new energy in Ethan. His movements were light, purposeful, even as he hung up his clothes. He caught her eye in the mirror and smiled, one that reached all the way to her heart. She could feel love radiating from him—this newfound commitment to living fully, this readiness for whatever lay ahead. Her heart swelled with gratitude.

CATALYST SIX

AMPLIFY YOUR FINANCES

"Your relationship with money is a reflection of your relationship with power. Transform one, and you transform both."
~Barbara Huson

Mirabel couldn't wait to share her latest revelations with Maya. During a quick phone call, she needed to ask for some guidance about her mother's latest financial crisis.

"Ethan and I had a wonderful time at the cabin—we rekindled our connection. We also hosted the most amazing party for our friends. But on the drive home from our getaway, my mother called with another money emergency. It brought up all my old money wounds."

She detailed her history with her mother's chronic financial struggles, frustration rising in her voice. "She's the source of my own money issues, and now she expects me to help. It's not fair!"

"I hear your pain," Maya said. "But holding onto resentment keeps you trapped in scarcity."

Mirabel sighed. "I get that but it's hard to let go when she started all this."

"Okay, before you can help her, I'd suggest considering some level of forgiveness—or at least seeing the past differently," Maya suggested.

"How about we use A.W.A.K.E. to shift your perspective? Are you up for trying that?" Maya asked.

"I'm up for anything! Let's do it."

As Maya guided her through Awareness, Willingness, Appreciation, Kindness, and Embodiment, tears rolled down Mirabel's cheeks. She realized something profound: her mother wasn't just "bad with money"—she had never learned how to manage it. As her intuition came forth, she spoke about what she was feeling to Maya.

"All these years," Mirabel began, her voice trembling, "I've been so angry at her. But she was doing the best she could with what she knew." She wiped her eyes with the back of her hand. "How could she teach me what no one had taught her?"

Maya's calm presence seemed to reach through the phone, creating a space for Mirabel's revelation to land fully. "That's a powerful insight, Mirabel. What else emerges for you as you sit with this understanding?"

Mirabel took a deep breath, feeling the weight of generations shifting and releasing within her. "It's like... I'm seeing her struggles through new eyes. The shame she must have carried, the anxiety every time bills came due." Her fingers twisted in her lap. "And I've been carrying that too, without even realizing it."

"The patterns we inherit," Maya said softly, "they run deep. But awareness is the first step towards change."

Mirabel nodded, feeling both lighter and heavier at once. "I think... I think I'm ready to break this cycle. Not just for me, but for her too. Maybe it's not too late for either of us to learn."

"Your mother did her best with what she knew," Maya said softly. "And forgiveness isn't about excusing her choices—it's about freeing yourself. When you release that burden, you both can have your own money journey without judgement and shame. Go ahead and take a big deep breath and when you release your breath know you are letting it go from all parts of you. From the past, the present and the future. Releasing all the energy from your mind, body and emotions. Let it go, freely and fully."

With each exhale, she felt the releasing of feelings from the past, as much as she could. Maya waited for a little while before she spoke again.

"How does that feel?"

"It feels really good. And I think I've gone into my head a bit...I want to help her, but I'm also afraid of falling back into old patterns," she whispered.

"When helping your mother, listen to your internal voice," she said. "Notice when it isn't criticizing you nor others. Listen to the voice when it's loving and supportive, even when things are hard. You can trust this voice."

"But," Maya added, "you might hear other messages too. These often come from fear. They might make you worry about losing control or facing the unknown or something else. These critical thoughts can make you feel guilty or want to protect yourself. Remember, these aren't your true self talking. It's okay to feel scared sometimes, but don't let fear control you."

Mirabel felt puzzled. "Wait a minute. I thought the critical voice in my head was helping me. It keeps me out of trouble. Are you saying there's supposed to be a different voice inside me that's kind and loving? I'm not sure I understand."

"The voice you want to cultivate speaks with kindness and belief in your potential," Maya confirmed. "It celebrates your strengths and sees the best in you and others, even during struggles. This supportive internal voice is the one that will guide you towards personal fulfillment."

She continued, "Listening to this voice encourages expansion. It counters fear-driven thoughts. For your mom's situation, ask yourself how to support her with love."

"It's natural to have doubts, but faith and commitment are necessary. This skill develops with practice and patience," Maya concluded.

Mirabel responded gratefully, "Thank you. I guess I have been learning how to pay attention to my thoughts as a result of what you're showing me."

"Beautiful. Now that you're improving this relationship with your inner voice, I think we're ready for Catalyst 6—Amplify Your Finances. I know you've tried to help your mom with money management before..."

Mirabel tensed at the memory. "Yeah, that didn't go so well. She got defensive, and I probably came across as judgmental. I don't want to repeat that mistake."

"Exactly," Maya nodded. "But now you have something different to work with. As you've been seeing, inner work isn't only for personal growth. It can change how you approach sensitive talks with your family."

"So you think there's actually a way to talk about money that won't push her away?" Mirabel asked, a mix of skepticism and hope in her voice.

"When you approach it with love, not frustration, she's likely to respond differently," Maya said. "You can't make anyone change, but you can learn to create a safer space for these discussions. Given how urgent this is, could we meet again in a few days? I want to explore some approaches that helped my clients in similar situations."

"I'd really like that," Mirabel said, opening her eyes wide. The old frustration was still there, but it was softer now, tempered by their conversation.

Maya's voice became resolute. "Remember, change happens step by step, with patience and compassion. Take your time. Go easy on yourself and your mom."

After ending the call, Mirabel sat back and let her body settle, her breath guiding her into a meditation. The worry about her mother's finances still weighed on her, but it felt different now—lighter, more manageable. Perhaps this shift was all she needed to build a bridge between them instead of a wall.

In the few days that followed, she found extra time to meditate and focused on forgiveness—for herself, her mom, and she even felt a nudge to consider forgiving her father. As she felt less tension and more calm, she sent a text to her mom to find a time they could meet right after her next session with Maya. They settled on having tea at her mom's house.

Mirabel settled into her couch for her session with Maya and took in a deep breath. The meditation of the past few days had helped calm her nerves, but she still felt a flutter of anticipation. As Maya appeared on screen, she smiled, ready to learn how to bridge this gap with her mother.

"How are you feeling about your upcoming visit with your mom?"

"Nervous, but ready," Mirabel replied. "The meditation has helped. I keep reminding myself this isn't about fixing everything at once."

"That's exactly right. Before we get into specific approaches, I'd like to share something with you."

"You know," she began, "thirty years ago, I was that attorney working endless hours. I drove a beat-up Toyota while my partners drove sports cars." She smiled at the memory. "Everyone thought I was missing out. I was making a partner's salary but living like a first-year associate. I was pouring most of my savings into rental properties in up-and-coming neighborhoods. I learned early the difference between wants and needs. Since needs were less expensive than wants, I focused there. And I knew that if I 'wanted' to retire early, I 'needed' to control my spending."

Mirabel leaned forward, curious to learn more about how Maya had retired so early.

"I had this dream of freedom by age 45," Maya continued. "And I got there—but I learned something important along the way. Yes, I'd achieved financial independence, but I'd missed out on so much life.

That's why I do this work now. Because you can build wealth without sacrificing joy."

"These past few months, you've been learning this balance. Now, let me show you what I've discovered about making money work for you while living fully in the present. This is how we'll activate the Sixth Catalyst—Amplifying Your Finances."

Maya paused, letting her personal story settle before shifting into mentor mode. "Everyone starts from a different place with money. I didn't come from wealth. But what I've discovered is that understanding how money works can improve anyone's life, regardless of where they begin."

"I've developed two sets of guidelines over the years—five key strategies and five fundamental rules. They're not complex financial theories, Mirabel. They're real lessons, ones I've lived. You can adapt each to your unique situation." Her eyes crinkled with warmth. "And remember—this isn't about comparing yourself to others. It's about finding your own path to financial freedom."

"Let's start with the strategies," Maya said, with the quiet confidence of someone who had walked this path before. "Ready?"

Mirabel nodded, settling in with her journal open.

"Perfect," Maya smiled. "These five strategies aren't just theory—they're the exact steps I used to supercharge my own income and build real wealth. And more importantly, they're the steps that have helped my clients transform their financial lives. I'll share some of their stories—real examples that show how these principles work in practice."

"Strategy 1: Increase Your Income. Building wealth begins with boosting earnings—you have to increase how much money you bring in. Take Jessica, a graphic designer at a small agency. Instead of waiting for raises, she took on weekend freelance projects. Within a year, her expanded portfolio landed her a job at a prestigious firm, doubling her salary. There are many ways to increase your income—the key is being creative."

"Strategy 2: Know Your Value," Maya emphasized. "While growing skills is important, knowing what they command in compensation is crucial. Take Mark, a software developer who researched market rates for his expertise. Armed with data showing comparable positions paying 20% more, he successfully negotiated a raise during his annual review. I also had an income breakthrough when I was practicing law and realized my expertise was worth premium rates."

"Strategy 3: Advocate for Yourself." Maya's voice grew passionate. "Don't expect handouts; champion your own interests! Jessica, a marketing manager, was consistently delivering outstanding results but felt undervalued. Instead of waiting for recognition, she compiled a detailed report of her achievements and requested a meeting with her boss. Her proactive approach led to a promotion and a significant pay increase. Start tracking your wins today—document your successes, gather testimonials or case studies, and build the case for your capabilities."

"Strategy 4: Pay Yourself First," Maya explained. "Automatically route a portion of your income to investments before spending a dime. This strategy bypasses the common end-of-the-month lament, 'I have nothing left to save!'" Maya's air of authority was clear: "Money is like closet space in a house. You've heard how the amount of stuff you own expands to fit the space available? Well, your expenditures will expand to reach whatever money you have available. That's why it is great to take your savings out first and learn to live on what remains."

"Strategy 5: Embrace the Power of 'No.'" Maya smiled. "In negotiations, keep asking until you hear 'no.' This ensures you're getting paid what you're worth. Many people talk themselves down before they even start negotiating. Take Olivia, an online content creator. She asks for premium rates for her work and promotions. If clients always say yes, she knows she's charging too little. Remember—hearing 'no' means you've found the ceiling. Without it, you'll never know your true value in the market."

As Maya finished sharing these strategies, Mirabel looked down at her notes, her mind already racing with possibilities. She hadn't realized how many opportunities she'd been passing by, simply because they hadn't occurred to her.

"You know what's wild?" she said. "I've been so focused on saving money, I never thought about growing it like this." She glanced up at Maya. "Some of these strategies feel a little scary, but in a good way."

"That's how I felt when I bought my first rental property," Maya said. "The trick is don't do everything at once." She continued. "And remember, it's about finding the right balance—you want to enjoy your life today while still building for tomorrow. Pick one strategy that speaks to you—maybe the one that makes you a little nervous but excited at the same time. Start there. The rest will follow."

"Let's dive into the top five rules for supercharging your savings."

"Rule One: Embrace Long-Term Thinking." Maya explained how starting early, even with small amounts, can lead to significant savings. "Saving $100 a month from age 18 could grow to over $200,000 by 65, thanks to compound interest! And if you start now, saving an extra $500 a month until 65, with an 8 percent annual return, you could have nearly $750,000 saved. The key is to start wherever you are—it's never too little or too late."

"Rule Two: Track Your Money," Maya said. "Think of it like being a money detective. When I first started as a young lawyer, I was making good money but had no idea where it was going. Once I started tracking every dollar, I discovered I was spending hundreds each month on takeout during late nights at the office. That awareness helped me make different choices. Know where every dollar comes from and goes—it's not about judgment, it's about awareness. My motto is to always spend less than you earn."

"Rule Three: Be Discerning. The goal is to spend more on what matters to you," Maya advised. "Maybe it's a dream vacation or those painting classes you've been eyeing. But here's the trick—cut back on things that don't bring you immense joy. For instance, cooking at home because you love it instead of eating out. It's about maximizing enjoyment while minimizing unnecessary expenses."

"Rule Four: Choose Experiences Over Stuff. After I retired, I realized how easy it was to spend money on things I didn't really need, just because I had it," Maya reflected. "The truth is, the joy from buying things fades quickly, but the memories from experiences last forever. When I look back now, I don't remember the designer suits I wore to court—I remember the weekend trips with friends, the cooking classes I took, the small moments that brought real joy. That's why I urge you to invest in memorable experiences, not in things."

"Rule Five: Avoid Keeping Up with the Joneses. Focus on your own financial goals and priorities to tune out the noise," Maya emphasized. "During my law career, I watched partners drain their wealth on luxury homes, vacations, and cars. By choosing differently, I achieved early retirement and financial freedom. To resist comparison pressure, institute a 'cooling-off' period for major purchases. Whether your threshold is $50 or $500, wait 72 hours before buying. This pause helps align spending with your values rather than social pressures or emotional purchases."

"Now I know that's a lot of information to absorb."

"It's okay. These strategies for boosting income and savings are great. They get me thinking about all kinds of possibilities," Mirabel said. "But I can't help wondering—is there a limit to how much we can do in the next few years?"

"Great question. It's important to remember that this is a holistic process. When I was practicing law, I discovered that having a clear goal for my money helped me stay focused. Every two years, I'd save enough to buy another small house in an up-and-coming neighborhood. It wasn't glamorous—these were modest homes that needed work—but it gave my savings a purpose. And my actions were compounding wealth over time."

Maya continued, "Having that clear goal changed my relationship with money. It wasn't about denying myself things—it was about working toward something bigger. Remember, this process is a marathon, not a sprint. With these strategies as your guide, you'll be amazed at how far you can go. Stay consistent, keep learning, and be patient."

Mirabel then asked, "What is the relationship between money and freedom? Sometimes I feel like no matter how much we earn and save, it's never going to be enough."

"Freedom is an internal feeling, not just about how much money you have. Freedom is a mindset, while wealth is a goal you work towards. When you feel you have enough, you're more likely to create a rich life which also leads to greater feelings of freedom."

"That's precisely why freedom can't be measured in dollars," Maya continued. "True freedom is the chance to be better, to live better. It's about having the space to grow, to learn, to become more fully yourself. Money can provide opportunities, yes, but it's what you do with those opportunities that matters."

Maya was encouraging. "When we chase money endlessly, we're often running away from something rather than toward something meaningful. But when we focus on growth, on becoming better versions of ourselves, we find a different kind of wealth—-one that no market crash can take away. All said, I'm thrilled to see you taking these steps toward financial empowerment. It will make a lasting difference for you and Ethan, and your mom too."

As the call ended, Mirabel closed her laptop and leaned back, emotions swirling. The tools Maya had given her felt powerful and transformative. Yet the thought of sharing them with her mother made her stomach tighten. Years of scarcity thinking weren't going to dissolve in a single conversation. Yet, for the first time, she saw both her mother's struggles and her own through clearer eyes. Taking a breath, Mirabel felt the familiar tension between hope and doubt, but this time, hope was winning.

Mirabel drove to her mother's apartment, buoyed by her fresh perspective yet aware of the delicate conversation ahead. She'd decided to tackle Sheena's financial troubles alone this time—Ethan's well-meaning advice had only created tension in the past. As familiar streets passed by, she felt both hopeful and nervous about the discussion to come.

She reflected on how much working on forgiveness had changed her perspective. She now saw her mother as a fellow human doing her best. That felt huge.

Sheena greeted her with a tired smile, her graceful features and luminous complexion reflecting her years of professional skincare expertise.

Her dark hair fell in soft waves around her face, expertly styled despite the day's pressures. Even with fatigue shadowing her eyes, she carried herself with natural elegance.

They sat in her mom's kitchen, where years of thoughtful touches had transformed the top floor rental into a sanctuary. The late afternoon sun illuminated the South San Francisco hills.

Mirabel placed an orchid on the small table. "Mom, I brought this for you. The green flowers symbolize harmony and health—a reminder of the positive changes we're about to make together."

Her mom kissed her cheek and admired the orchid as she poured them both a cup of tea. "It's pretty," she said, touching a petal. "Thank you."

They sat down and Mirabel touched her mom's shoulder.

"I know you're struggling with money," she began softly. "I want to help, just the two of us."

Sheena's shoulders slumped. "I just don't know what to do anymore. I'm drowning in debt."

"Mom, I hear you. I've been learning about managing money. You're spending more than you're bringing in—is that right?"

"I guess so. I've always been this way. I can't change..." Sheena crossed her arms, her cheeks flushing. "I don't know why we're having this conversation again."

"Mom, there's no need to be—"

"I'm not embarrassed," Sheena cut in, standing abruptly and turning away. "I'm tired of feeling like I'm your project to fix."

Mirabel took a steady breath. "You're not a project, Mom. You're my mother, and I love you. I hate seeing you stressed like this."

"Well, I hate being stressed," She said, her back still turned. "But I also hate feeling like a failure every time we have one of these conversations."

"You're not a failure, Mom," Mirabel said softly. "Look how you built your skincare business from nothing. Your clients adore you."

"That's different," She replied, gesturing at her pile of unopened bills, their red "Past Due" stamps stark in the afternoon light. "I can do facials, make people feel beautiful. But this?" She scrunched her nose and shook her head. "I had to put supplies on credit just to keep working."

"Mom, you taught me about persistence when I was struggling in my past jobs. Now let me help you apply that same determination to your finances. We'll do this together, step by step."

Sheena's shoulders relaxed slightly and she turned back to the table and sat down again. "What if..." she paused, stirring her tea. "What if we look at everything and it's worse than I thought? Sometimes I lie awake at night wondering if I should just give it all up. Get some normal job with benefits. Have some security."

"Is that what you want? To give up your business?"

"No," she whispered, her eyes filling with tears. "My clients are like family. But I'm so tired of this constant stress about money."

"Then let's start there," she said gently. "Not with giving up, but with making your business work better for you."

After a long moment, her mom sighed. "I just always focused on the beauty part... the business part scares me."

"First," Mirabel continued, "we need to get a clear picture of your income and expenses. Have you written down all of your monthly bills and compared them to your income?"

"Not really. I just kind of... wing it each month."

"That's okay," Mirabel reassured her. "It's a starting point. Why don't we start a list right now? We can categorize your expenses and see where your money is going."

As they began to work on the list, Sheena's tension eased. "You know, I've always been afraid to look at the numbers closely. It felt easier to just ignore it."

Mirabel smiled, catching her tendency to judge her mom. "That's really common, Mom. A lot of people feel that way about money," she said. "But knowledge is power. Once we have a clear picture of your finances, we can start making a plan together. The important thing is, we're taking this step together."

"I never thought I'd be getting financial advice from my daughter," She chuckled.

As her mom refilled their teacups, Mirabel continued gently, "Okay, I'll start by explaining that there are two main ways to solve this problem. One is to cut expenses to reduce debt. The other is to adopt an abundance mindset to increase income and opportunities.""

"What do you mean by 'cutting expenses to reduce debt'?"

Mirabel took a sip of tea and explained, "It's what Ethan and I have been doing for a while now. We focus on reducing our spending as much as possible to pay off our debts. You know, things like moving to a cheaper place, selling one of our cars, eating out less, or buying the cheapest groceries. The idea is to cut back as much as you can to free up money to put towards your debts."

Sheena shrugged her shoulders. "I've been trying to do that, but it never seems to be enough."

Mirabel looked at her. "Right. I've been realizing the same thing. While cutting back can help in the short term, it's hard to get ahead in life by only focusing on having less. It hasn't helped us stop worrying about money. Plus, with rising prices, even if you keep cutting back, your money doesn't go as far as it used to."

Her entire body slumped. "So, what's the alternative?"

"That's where this new mindset comes in," Mirabel replied with a smile. "I've been learning that instead of just focusing on spending less, Ethan and I also look for ways to expand, by earning more and creating new opportunities. It's about believing there's always room for growth and improvement in your financial situation."

She furrowed her brow. "That sounds nice, but how does it work in practice?"

"Well, depending on your situation, it could mean learning new skills for higher cost treatments, expanding on what you already do, or finding creative ways to earn extra income. The key is focusing on making more money, not just cutting your expenses." Mirabel explained.

"I see," she mused, sipping her tea. "It's a different way of looking at things, isn't it?"

"Most definitely. And while it might take more effort to start, it has the potential to improve your financial situation in the long run."

"It's a new mindset I'm learning about." Mirabel shared calmly. "Instead of focusing on what you lack, you start by considering how you can create more. You ask yourself, 'How can I be kind to myself, so I am motivated to put in the time and energy to grow and improve? What can I do to generate more income coming into my life?' It's about shifting your mindset from scarcity to possibility."

Sheena looked intrigued. "Hmmm."

"The foundation of abundant thinking is that there's more than enough available and you just have to figure out how to tap into it. In your case, you already have great skills and a loyal customer base. You can do many things to raise your income. You need to think creatively and act."

Mirabel added, "For example, mom, you could raise your prices. Or you could introduce new products. The new products will encourage clients to visit more often. Or you could expand your business through advertising. You could also ask current clients to refer you to their friends and family."

"You could rent your space to another esthetician on your off days, or hire someone to offer extra services," she suggested. "It's about growing what you already have."

Sheena sat back, considering. "Part of me wants to try this because it matters to you, and part of me is just tired of struggling. I've been so focused on surviving, I never thought about growing my business."

She rubbed the top of her mom's forearm. "I can't solve this for you, but I can help explore options and connect you with resources."

They sat quietly as she studied Maya's handouts, asking questions about income and savings.

"Mindset," Sheena repeated thoughtfully. "Mindset."

"Honey, I love what you're trying to help me do here," She said tearfully, "but at 57 with little savings, I wonder if it's too late."

"Mom, I understand how daunting this feels.... but starting now can mean a completely different life in five years. People have rebuilt everything in less time. With your dedication and my support, you can create real financial security. I love you, and together, who knows what we can achieve? You can do this." She said encouragingly.

Sheena smiled through tears. "I love you too. Having you in my corner means everything. I'll need your help... probably a lot of it. But for the first time, this makes me think about a life beyond just surviving. What I'm hearing you say is that I can increase my income, build some savings, and make better choices. And when that happens I won't have to feel so trapped anymore?"

Just stating these possibilities out loud overwhelmed her, and she broke down sobbing. Mirabel got up to hold her mother through this release, recognizing the same raw vulnerability she'd experienced in her own recent emotional breakthroughs.

After a few minutes Sheena pulled away, wiping her eyes quickly and looking flustered. "Oh goodness, I'm sorry—I don't know what came over me. Let me just..." She took a shaky breath, trying to compose herself. "Thank you. Now let's work on what's next."

Looking directly into her mother's eyes knowing she was uncomfortable with showing emotion, Mirabel said, "Mom, it's okay. I'm here and I want to help you. I need this too. I have a lot to learn just like you. We have time to do this right."

Sheena tried to smile, tears welling up again. "Thank you. Thank you."

They spent the next hour at the kitchen table. Mirabel helped her mother sort through receipts and bills, creating categories on a yellow legal pad. They found small wins. They consolidated salon product orders for better discounts. They adjusted her booking schedule to maximize profits. They found a new cheaper phone plan.

With each solution that didn't require her daughter's financial intervention, Sheena's entire being transformed. Tension melted from her shoulders. Her voice grew stronger as she contributed ideas, drawing on business instincts she hadn't realized she possessed.

It felt like a real path forward.

"Thank you," her mom said again, reaching across to squeeze Mirabel's hand, her voice wavering. "Not only for the help, but for believing in me when I couldn't see it myself."

Mirabel grinned. "I'm starting classes to learn about managing money, and I'd love for you to join me. We can learn together, side by side." She explained an online app that helps manage finances. It teaches users to give every dollar a purpose: pay off debt and save more.

Sheena's face brightened. "Could I use it to get my bills under control?"

"Yes, but I want to be honest and say it's not going to be easy, it'll take trial and error. But when you keep trying, that's when you'll see real changes." She explained, "Through all of this I'm learning to be kinder to myself. We both have harsh inner critics. Changing that voice could make a huge difference in how you approach all of this."

Sheena sighed. "I've been so focused on what's missing that I couldn't see a way through." She wiped her eyes, then asked, "Could Sarah join us too? You know she struggles with money like I do. Maybe this could bring us closer?"

Warmth spread through Mirabel's chest. "Absolutely! We can all learn the budgeting app together and support each other. How about a weekly money date—the three of us—to share what we're learning?"

On the drive home, her mind raced with possibilities. Helping her mother and sister turn their situations around gave her a sense of purpose. Learning together would make the journey more meaningful.

As she pulled into the driveway, Ethan was waiting on the front steps.

"How did it go?" He asked, opening his arms to give her a hug.

"It went surprisingly well!" She replied, hugging him back. "Mom was receptive to the ideas about managing her money differently. We're going to invite Sarah to join us too. I'm encouraged that this could really help her and me too!"

He nodded supportively. "Sounds like real progress."

Settling into bed later, Mirabel reflected on the day. Her new strength had opened a path to real understanding with her mother, and maybe even with her sister. She drifted off, excited for the future, looking forward to the changes they would make together.

NAVIGATE DECISIONS

"Every decision is a commitment to a path. The key isn't choosing perfectly, but learning perfectly from each choice."
~Mellody Hobson

Early evening light filled the room as Mirabel sat at her computer for her session with Maya.

"You're glowing!" Maya said when her face appeared onscreen.

"I feel so lucky," Mirabel replied. "Ethan and I have been talking about creating a more purposeful life."

"Tell me more."

"We want to focus on what brings us joy," she explained. "Ethan's making a list of new things to try—qualifying for a triathlon, skydiving with friends. He's committed to figuring out what makes him happy."

"What about you? What have you discovered?"

"I'm finding joy in things that don't cost much," she explained. "I've started painting again after a six-year break. A few weeks ago, I dug out some old canvases and paints I had stored away. When I posted one of the pieces on Instagram, a friend offered to buy it for $500! That covered all my supplies to really get back into it. Plus, I'm taking money classes with Mom. It's amazing how joy can show up when you least expect it."

"That's incredible! Good for you."

"Ethan and I have been spending more time with friends who share our values."

"How so?"

"Well, instead of expensive restaurants, we do potlucks. Game nights. Hiking." Her eyes lit up. "It's funny, but I'm noticing all these small moments I used to miss. And the more I value myself, the better my life feels."

"That's great to hear. And how about your mom? Last time we spoke, you were worried about her."

"Oh! That conversation with Mom was so powerful." Mirabel pulled out her phone, scrolling through her messages. "I have all these texts from her. She's making real changes, even though it's not easy. Small steps every day." She held up her phone, beaming. "See? She's actually tracking her expenses now!"

"It's amazing how one conversation can spark such powerful changes."

"It really is," she said, tucking her phone away. "Actually, that reminds me of what's happening at work. Things have really shifted since... you know, the fiasco."

"I'd love to hear about it." Maya leaned forward.

"Well, I've been meeting regularly with my team and my boss about the new product launch. But here's the interesting part—" Mirabel paused. "Remember how I got into trouble at work?"

Maya nodded.

"It turns out I wasn't the only one. They uncovered this whole pattern of managers taking credit for their teams' work." Mirabel's eyes brightened. "And you won't believe this—Aisha actually used what happened with me as a catalyst. She and other leaders are committed to changing the entire company culture."

"Wow," Maya said. "From almost getting fired to helping transform the company. That's quite a turn."

"I know, right?" she smiled. "It's like once I started being more transparent with my team, it created this ripple effect. The product launch actually feels exciting now, not stressful."

"Through this I've learned to focus on helping others instead of judging them. It feels great to live this way," she said.

"You've made incredible progress."

"I feel like I'm making some real shifts in this abundance work... what do you think?" Mirabel asked after a pause.

"Yes and there's only 'right' for you," Maya replied. "This journey is yours to customize. You'll know its working when you feel expansive, though temporary constriction is natural. Life flows between expansion and contraction—embrace both. We're building better ways to navigate life, not seeking perfection. Does that resonate?"

"Yes," Mirabel nodded. "I can see how my old habits of self-judgment try to creep back in."

"I think you're now ready to address one of your initial questions: how to make decisions that lead to living a more joyful life."

Mirabel perked up, remembering.

"Making good decisions is crucial, especially regarding money and resources," Maya continued. "It's not just about numbers but aligning choices with your values and vision. Your decisions can have a big impact on your life."

Mirabel nodded her head in agreement.

"Today, we're going to explore the Seventh Catalyst—Navigating Decisions."

"With money choices, people often swing between pure intuition and endless analysis. But there's a middle path, one that can serve you for years to come. Would you like to know what that looks like?"

"Yes, please."

"I've found that a balanced approach works best," Maya continued. "It's about combining practical thinking with your intuition. This way, you're not ignoring your gut feelings, but you're also not overlooking important facts."

"Remember, this is just the beginning. We'll take it step by step, and you don't need to master it all at once. The goal is to make choices that align with your values without feeling overwhelmed which can put you back in a fear-based state."

"Where do we start?" Mirabel asked, feeling at ease.

"This is my simple three-step process. The first step is Prepare," Maya began. "Before any big decision, it's crucial to gather all the facts you need. Make sure you have complete information by doing research if necessary. Don't rush this step. A solid understanding is key to a wise decision. Once you've collected all the relevant information, take a moment to breathe and center yourself. This combination of being well-informed and calm sets the stage for the next step."

"That makes sense," Mirabel confirmed. "It's like creating a foundation for a house."

"Next is Reflect and Decide," Maya continued. "This is where you turn inward. Use techniques like A.W.A.K.E. to ground yourself. Face any fears that may be affecting your decision. Then, revisit your 'I am' statements to ensure you're empowered."

"Once you've reflected, trust yourself to make the decision. Remember, you can always learn and adjust as you go. The important thing is to move forward with confidence."

Mirabel nodded.

"The final step is Act," she explained. "Use your intuition, guided by the facts and insights you've gained. Once you've decided, take a small, immediate action to set things in motion. This builds momentum and commitment."

"That makes sense," she said, feeling inspired. "I will definitely put this approach to good use."

"Great," Maya replied. "And remember, after you act, pay attention to what happens. Be ready to review and adjust your course when needed. Flexibility is key to good decision making."

"This process is the basis for something bigger—what many call manifesting. In the self-help world, people often rush to 'manifest'. They ignore some crucial groundwork. That's why I've taken the time to teach you how to approach decisions mindfully from the start."

"You and Ethan are already manifestors, whether you realize it or not. You've been shaping your reality all your lives. Now, with these tools, you can do it more intentionally," Maya concluded.

Mirabel felt energized by these new insights.

As the call ended, she was eager to share what she'd learned with Ethan. She imagined them applying these tools together, tackling their future with a shared sense of purpose and clarity.

Her mind felt so open. What decisions would they make differently now? How might their lives change as they applied these new approaches?

With a mix of excitement and curiosity, Mirabel knew challenges would come, but now she felt better equipped to face them—not alone, but as a team with Ethan.

The sound of her sister's laughter drifted through the window as Mirabel walked up to her mother's home, a bouquet cradled in her arms. She savored the moment. It had been months since she'd heard that sound.

When she'd first called Sarah about joining their money date, she had been hesitant. "I don't think I can do what you and Mom are doing," Sarah had said. "All that budgeting and planning... It's overwhelming. But..." There was a long pause. "I miss spending time with you both. So maybe I can just come and listen?"

"That's perfect," Mirabel had assured her. "Just be there with us."

Now, stepping inside, Mirabel found herself in a subtly transformed space. The pile of unopened bills that usually cluttered the kitchen counter was gone, replaced by a neat folder labeled "Monthly Budget."

Through the doorway, she could see Sarah sitting cross-legged on the living room floor, her laptop open to the budgeting app, dark curls pulled back in a messy bun that made her look so much like their mother.

"I'll be right there!" Mirabel called out, heading to the kitchen for a vase. As she arranged the flowers—roses, lilies, and daisies mingling their scents—she could hear her mom and sister's quiet conversation from the other room. The familiar sound made her pause with emotion. This was everything she'd hoped for.

She carried the vase to the kitchen table, grabbed her laptop and joined them in the living room.

"Okay," Mirabel said, settling onto the couch. "The first step is just getting clear on where our money is actually going. Mom, you started this last week—how did it feel to start tracking everything?"

"Intimidating at first," Sheena admitted, "but then it became almost like a game. I had no idea how much I was spending on little things throughout the day."

"Oh, that's great! Can you believe how much there is to learn?" Mirabel asked. "It's uncomfortable and challenging, but we're actually facing this stuff which feels good."

"What about you, Sarah?" Mirabel asked gently. "What made you want to join us today?"

Sarah shifted uncomfortably, glancing at her laptop screen. "Remember what I said on the phone? I'm mostly here to be with you two." She tucked a loose curl behind her ear. "But... I guess I'm also tired of not knowing where my money goes each month. Even with this new job, I'm still living paycheck to paycheck."

"That's actually a great place to start," Mirabel said. "Just being aware. No pressure to change anything yet."

"Right," Sarah said skeptically. "No pressure." But she leaned forward slightly as Mirabel opened the app. "So how exactly does it all work?"

Mirabel smiled, recognizing her sister's familiar pattern—resistance followed by curiosity. "Let me show you how it divides everything into categories. We can start by just tracking spending for a week—no judgments, just awareness." She moved closer to help Sarah set up her first digital envelope.

"Should we watch the next training video?" Mirabel asked, pulling up her laptop and glancing in the direction of Sarah. "This one walks through the envelope system in detail. But we can walk through it together if you'd prefer?"

"Let's do the videos," Sarah stated as she tucked her legs under the coffee table.

They sat close together as Mirabel pressed play. Sarah sat back and listened, typing notes into her computer as the instructor explained how to categorize expenses and assign a purpose to every dollar. Sheena found herself dividing her attention between the screen and Sarah's reaction.

"Those are really good notes, honey," Sheena said with a sheepish smile. "Would you mind sharing them with me?"

"Of course, Mom," Sarah replied.

"I like how they explain it's not about restriction," Sheena said when the video ended. "It's about knowing where your money is going."

"And these videos are available anytime, right?" Sarah asked, clicking through the library. "There's so much here and so little time..."

Sheena nodded, a proud smile on her face. "I just have to tell you both how much I love all of this! What you told me last time, Mirabel, is making such a difference in my business. Since we met I tested raising my prices, gained a few new clients and added some new treatments. I've already brought in an extra $1,000 this month."

Mirabel's jaw dropped and Sarah exclaimed, "That's incredible! You're really doing it, Mom!"

Mirabel grinned and said, "Wow!"

Sheena laughed, "And you know what? My clients didn't even complain. A few even said it was about time I charged what my services were worth. Which means I will raise my prices for all of my clients next week!"

"I'm glad to hear it," Mirabel said smiling. "It's because your clients appreciate how good you are at what you do."

She couldn't help but feel inspired. She knew that, by focusing on what they wanted, her mom and eventually her sister could better manage their money and save more.

"Oh, and get this," Sheena added, her eyes wide with disbelief. "Remember that skin care machine I invested in years ago that didn't work like they had said it would? Well, there was a class action suit, and I received a check in the mail the other day for $10,000!"

Mirabel gasped. "That's amazing! What are you going to do with the money?"

"First off, that 72-hour rule about impulse buying works," Sheena grinned. "For the first time, I feel in control. I'm using fifty percent to pay down debt, thirty percent for emergency savings, and most of the rest to improve my business. I even set aside a little for a weekend trip with friends. It feels wonderful to make better choices."

"I need to try that rule," Sarah admitted, typing a note on her computer. "Do you think it could help me kick my ten-dollar coffee habit?"

Sheena's laugh was warm and understanding. "Honey, I'm not sure any rule can cure a coffee and sugar addiction. Sorry! But I am learning to focus on what truly fulfills me, like my love of beauty. Maybe for you it's not about giving up coffee entirely, but finding ways to make it more special when you do have it?"

"It's definitely a different way of thinking," Sarah said skeptically.

Mirabel watched her mother, stunned at the transformation. The woman who once spent hours complaining about circumstances was now embracing life's imperfections and trying not to judge her daughters. The change had happened quickly yet felt real.

"Mom, I'm glad you're doing better," Mirabel said proudly. "I've found that not being so hard on myself helps me focus on what's important. Is it the same for you?"

Sheena's voice was thick with emotion. "It is. If you weren't leading the way, I wouldn't be here. You've inspired me."

Sarah looked between them, wonder in her expression. "It's amazing watching you both. I always thought money talks had to end in stress and arguments. This feels... nice."

They sat together in comfortable silence, each reflecting on their journey—Sheena embracing change, Mirabel lighting the way, and Sarah taking a few first steps. They had discovered something precious: a new way to face challenges together.

"Same time next week?" Sarah asked as she gathered her things, hugging them both goodbye. "Who knew talking about money could actually bring us closer?"

On her drive home, Mirabel reflected on Sarah and her mother's growing financial confidence—how they were both embracing abundance in their own ways. Her thoughts then drifted to Ethan. *Maybe this is what they needed all along—me finally seeing money as a tool rather than a measuring stick. It feels so much better this way.* As she pulled into her driveway, a smile played across her lips—this felt like the beginning of something extraordinary.

On a quiet Sunday evening, Mirabel and Ethan sat in their living room, surrounded by the warm glow of the setting sun. Maya's diagrams and process maps lay scattered on the coffee table, while Mirabel's journal sat open beside them.

Ethan settled back into the couch. "You know, we've been talking about having a baby on and off for what, almost a year now?" He absently traced the rim of his glass. "And I've got to say, what you've been sharing is helping me get more serious about it."

"Me too," she said softly.

"I was thinking..." he continued. "Maybe we could use her decision process together? You know, to figure out if now might be the right time to seriously think about having a baby?"

A flush of warmth spread across her cheeks. "Yeah, I'd really like that." She reached for the list among the papers. They studied Maya's three steps:

<u>Guide for Navigating Decisions</u>

Prepare: Gather information and center yourself

Reflect and Decide: Turn inward, face fears, trust yourself

Act: Move forward with small, immediate steps

They paused to take a breath together, the tension melting from their shoulders. Mirabel placed the paper on her lap. "For step one, 'Prepare,' let's look at what we know. Last week, I talked with our neighbors about their six-month-old son Jacob. They recommended some great local parenting groups and birthing classes. They also gave me some information about pediatricians in the area. I still need to look into it more but it got me started."

"Great," he agreed. "And we've discussed timing with our careers. Your company's parental leave is good, and my business is stable enough now that I can adjust my schedule. Me being self-employed could really help us with the flexibility we'd need."

The last rays of sunlight painted long shadows across the room as he continued. "And what about our finances—do you think we'd need to make some changes right away?"

"I've actually been secretly playing with some numbers over the past few days." she smiled and pulled her journal closer. "I wanted to see how our budget could accommodate the extra expenses of having a child. From what I can tell, we should be fine. We will need to adjust expenses a bit, but our home is perfect for starting a family and I feel like we can make it work."

She took another breath. "Ready for step two? For 'Reflect and Decide,' we need to acknowledge our fears and expectations about parenting. For me, I worry about balancing my career and personal life with the time commitment of raising a child." Her voice got quiet as she thought about her own childhood. "It's definitely something I'm willing to make time for. It's so important to be fully present for a child."

He squeezed her hand. "I agree. I've always dreamed of being a father. I know that raising a child should not be all about the money. It's about love and being there when they need us."

"We should also consider our current situation and future plans." she turned to face him fully. "How do you see a child fitting into our lives?"

"That's a good question." his expression thoughtful. "Our marriage is better than ever and our careers are established. I think we're in a good position to start a family."

The room had grown dim, but neither moved to turn on a light. In the growing twilight, Mirabel's voice was steady. "When I think about this decision, what comes to me is that I am ready to be a loving, kind parent. It aligns with my values and dreams and what I most want. What's coming up for you?"

"I am prepared to be a supportive father and partner." his voice certain. "It's something I've always wanted."

They took a moment to reflect, then looked at each other with confidence.

A smile spread across Mirabel's face. "We have our answer. We're ready to start a family."

Ethan squeezed her hand. "I agree. Now, for step three—'Act'. What's a small step we can take right away?" He grinned, wiggling his eyebrows.

She laughed, the sound bright in the darkening room. "How about scheduling a check-up with my doctor this week?"

"Perfect." he pulled her close, both of them feeling excitement about their decision and the promise of expanding their family. As they held each other in the gathering dusk, Mirabel felt her world expanding once again—this time, with the quiet certainty that came from choosing love over fear.

A little while later Mirabel's phone rang—it was Tanya.

"Hi! How are you?" Tanya asked.

"I'm fantastic. So much goodness is happening! What's up?"

"We're thrilled you're coming to the gala! Since we're nearly sold out, would you consider purchasing two additional tickets? It would mean a lot to us."

"Oh, wow, hold on, let me check with Ethan." Mirabel muted her phone. "Okay, it's Tanya. She said they are nearly sold out for their gala and she's asking us to buy two more tickets to help them reach their goal. We could take Leila and Stu if they're available. Would that be okay?"

After a thoughtful pause, Ethan simply said, "Yes, tell her okay."

Mirabel grinned—she was not expecting that response! "We'll take the two extra tickets," she told Tanya, who was overjoyed and grateful.

She hung up and turned to Ethan. "I know donating money isn't always easy for you, but I truly appreciate this. Tanya's work is so important."

"I know how much this means to you," he smiled. "I'm glad we can be a part of it."

Mirabel texted Leila and soon got her reply: "We'd love to join you! Count us in!"

The realization hit her then: she'd been caught up in her own concerns for too long, seeing everything through the lens of personal struggles. But Maya had opened her eyes to something bigger. The work had planted seeds that were now blooming in Mirabel's mind. She thought about the pure joy of giving gifts to friends, expecting nothing in return.

This shift felt especially meaningful as she contemplated becoming a mom and the instinct to put another's needs before your own. Perhaps this was a big life lesson—that true growth comes not only from looking inward, but also from helping others.

Catalyst Eight

Take Inspired Action

"Inspired action flows from alignment with your deepest truth. It's not about doing more, but doing what matters."

~Oprah Winfrey

The air was festive and celebratory. Mirabel, Ethan, Leila, and Stu entered the glittering ballroom for the annual gala fundraiser their friend Tanya was hosting — a far cry from their usual outings.

The room buzzed with excitement, filled with over 400 influential people from the Bay Area community. They were united in their support for the national nonprofit's mission to improve policies and systems affecting the reproductive lives of marginalized communities.

The couples exchanged warm greetings, celebrating their friendship and all that had happened in the past few months. The evening promised to be a special one, combining their desire to give back with the joy of shared experiences.

They mingled with other guests, sipping champagne and enjoying tasty hors d'oeuvres. As the evening progressed, Mirabel noticed Ethan reading the brochures with great interest, learning more about how the organization helped families and women overcome systemic challenges. He commented a few times about how impressive the nonprofit's work was.

Tanya took the stage to kick off the evening's main event, a live auction, and the room buzzed. As various items were presented and bid upon, the energy in the ballroom continued to build. Then the auctioneer announced an item that drew a gasp from Mirabel.

"Our next item is a romantic weekend getaway at the stunning Ahwahnee Hotel in Yosemite! This is the perfect chance for a couple to escape the busy city and reconnect with nature and each other. Shall we start the bidding at $1,000?"

The change happened in an instant.

Mirabel saw it flash across Ethan's face—that wild spark of inspiration she knew so well. His features softened, and in that moment, she read his mind: their late-night talks about Yosemite, her whispered dreams of misty waterfalls and granite peaks touching stars. Before she could react, his paddle shot up beside her like a starting gun.

Time stopped.

The first bid hit her like a physical force: "$1,500!" She watched, frozen, as his grin grew with every bid, his enthusiasm rolling off him in waves that only heightened her panic. Her heart hammered against her ribs as the numbers climbed: $2,500, $3,000, $3,500.

"Ethan, it's too much. We can't spend that kind of money," she urged, gripping his arm. But her words seemed to float away in the electric atmosphere of the auction room. She felt caught in a storm of contradictions—terror at the mounting sum, awe at his unwavering certainty, fear of what this meant for their future. The paddle kept rising, and with each bid, she felt herself being pulled under by a tide of overwhelming emotion.

Then, like a bolt of lightning cutting through storm clouds, clarity struck. In that electrifying moment, everything shifted. The source of her fear revealed itself—a deep wound that had never healed. Once money was spent, it would vanish forever, just like her father had. But as she reached to stop Ethan one final time, a profound realization washed over her like a cleansing rain. The truth shattered her chains, setting her spirit free.

Her focus on money fell away. She was awakening to the infinite power that had always resided within her, waiting to be discovered. Every time Ethan raised his paddle was now a transformative leap of faith, a testament to the life he knew they were both committed to. Her heart burst with the understanding that giving was never about losing. It was a pure expression of love... it was freedom.

In the crescendo of the bidding, Mirabel felt the suffocating grip of her fears dissolve. True living, she realized, meant opening her heart without reservation. It meant trusting in the flow of life, in its capacity to nurture and sustain. The ballroom, moments ago a battlefield of anxiety, now felt like sacred ground.

Ethan's final bid rang out like a revelation. They had started from different places, faced different obstacles, but here they stood united in their belief in life's fundamental goodness. In their trust in each other. In love's unerring ability to guide them home.

"Sold to #147 for $5,000!" The auctioneer's voice ignited a wave of cheers, the room's energy swelling to embrace their bold decision. Mirabel turned to Ethan, tears spilling freely as she pulled him close. The amount might have seemed modest to some, but for them, it was a profound investment in something larger than themselves.

Ethan couldn't have known the depths of her emotional break-through, but seeing her tears, he asked softly, "Are you okay?"

Mirabel's lips curved into a radiant smile, her eyes shining. "I've never been better," she replied.

Relief washing over Ethan's features. "Good," he said, giving her another hug. "We can always earn more, right?"

"Absolutely," Mirabel agreed. "That's true and I love every bit of what just happened."

As they embraced, Mirabel's voice quivered with raw emotion. She whispered, "Thank you for being my rock, my anchor in this storm. I love you. Thank you for showing me how much more there is to life."

Ethan smiled back at her with radiant love.

Leila and Stu watched with heartfelt smiles, happy to witness their friends' joy.

Later in the evening, Tanya approached Mirabel, a curious smile on her face. "What an incredible turn of events with Ethan tonight!

Can I assume something big has happened with him over the past few months?"

Mirabel laughed, her eyes sparkling with joy. "I'm just as surprised as you are. I had no idea. But I'm so grateful it happened here, while supporting you and your remarkable work. It takes me back to our first conversation after I got back from Paris. I know you weren't sure about where all of this was headed. But, witnessing what you're doing tonight is the epitome of abundant thinking. You believe in what's possible for others. Your work helps people in huge, life-changing ways."

Tanya nodded. "Thank you. You're right. Many people face obstacles in reaching their dreams. But that doesn't mean it's impossible. We'll do everything we can to help lift others up. It may not be perfect, but it means something for those we help."

As the night continued, the four friends shared stories, laughter, and ideas. Leila approached Mirabel and Ethan directly with a question. "You know, I've been giving more thought to my financial situation lately," Leila began. "I've saved for vacations, like our trip to Paris, and put money in my 401(k). But I feel ready to try investing on my own. Do you have any insights or recommendations to share?"

Ethan smiled with excitement. "I'd be more than happy to help you, Leila. I've been investing for more than 10 years, and I've learned a lot along the way. I can show you some of the cool things I've been doing with our investments."

"That'd be great! Thank you."

Leila turned to Mirabel and said, "You know, it's funny. When we were in Paris, I thought you had everything figured out already. I never imagined the conversations the two of us had would have such an impact on you."

She gave Leila a warm side-hug. "Your words and actions inspire me. You inspired changes I never thought possible. I'm so grateful for your friendship."

Leila's smile was huge as she replied. "I'm so happy I could be helpful to you."

As the gala celebration continued, Mirabel caught Ethan's eye across the room. They shared a knowing smile, acknowledging how far they'd come. She felt the pieces of their life together falling into place. As she took in her friends and the glittering event, a part of her wondered: *now that everything they'd wanted seemed within reach, I wonder what will happen next?*

In her sunlit living room, Mirabel settled into her final session with Maya, a vibrant purple orchid blooming beside her.

"I never expected all this growth when we started," Mirabel said. "I just wanted to enjoy life more."

Maya smiled. "I understand, and I'm curious: what have you discovered from our time together?"

"I've realized something profound," Mirabel began, her voice steady with newfound certainty. "Abundance doesn't come from playing it safe or hitting certain numbers. It's about refusing to live anything less than the life you know is possible for you. My views on money and freedom—they were inherited. From my family, my community, maybe even my ancestors. They weren't even my own, yet they've dictated how I live my life."

Maya nodded, pride illuminating her expression.

"Now I see challenges differently," Mirabel continued, her voice strong. "They're not obstacles—they're invitations to be myself. I've discovered that this journey is uniquely personal. Being true to what resonates is way more fulfilling than chasing society's version of success. When my choices align with the person I really am, that's when I feel truly wealthy."

Mirabel's eyes were bright with revelation. "But it goes so much deeper than just learning about having or being enough. You guided me into the cave of myself, Maya—into spaces I'd forgotten existed. Just illuminating them caused ripples of understanding. Sometimes the release was immediate—an 'oh' of recognition that dissolved the pattern instantly. Other times, it needed time to integrate."

She smiled, remembering. "The most transformative gift you gave me was your constant reminder: 'Don't make it wrong.' You'd ask what would happen if nothing was wrong here, if I could just be with whatever I found. That helped me begin to develop this beautiful way to self-reflect without judging myself. It showed me that living fully means embracing all of myself."

"You're embodying wisdom now, not just theory," Maya confirmed.

"That wisdom came from learning to see beauty in all of it," Mirabel replied. "Even the parts that seemed burned out. You taught me to be okay seeing it all, to follow the threads back out without judgment. It all goes back to self-compassion."

Mirabel paused, vulnerability softening her voice. "The journey hasn't been smooth. Even now, there are days when old doubts creep in—when I question if I'm enough. But the difference is, I now recognize these feelings as echoes of those beliefs about self-worth that I'm still working on."

Maya noted, "On difficult days, remember you have anchors—the practice of self-kindness, the love of those around you, the gratitude that's become your daily companion." She paused, letting her words settle. "Rewriting your money story, challenging those old beliefs about your worth—it takes tremendous courage. And time." A gentle smile touched her lips. "But you've already shown something remarkable: the strength to recognize what doesn't serve you anymore, and the wisdom to let it go."

"Through this process, I've learned to forgive—my mom, Ethan, and especially myself. Those old feelings of rejection that I've carried... I'm healing them now. And I've realized something—my father was doing his best too, just like all of us. I'm going to reach out to some relatives and see if they can help me connect with him. I don't have any expectations, but I'm ready to open that door. Just months ago, I wouldn't have thought this possible."

She continued, "Something extraordinary happened with Ethan at the gala." She paused, her gaze turning inward as she searched for the right words to describe a new thought. "When our eyes met, I felt myself unfurling like a flower. He didn't just see me—he witnessed every hidden part I'd tucked away since I was a kid. In his presence, I finally remembered what it meant to feel completely safe."

"Oh, Mirabel," Maya replied, her eyes glistening, "That's beautiful. I'm so happy for both of you. To be fully seen by the person you love is more rare than people may think. And hearing you speak about forgiveness... It's wonderful. And now, choosing to reach out to your father—that takes real courage. But you're right, you are ready. I can see it in your smile and hear it in your voice. If you take one thing from our time together, let it be this: you have become your own catalyst, and you have everything you need to live an extraordinary life."

Mirabel's entire being welled with emotion. "I need you to know what this journey has meant to me, Maya. You saw me—really saw me—when I couldn't even see myself. You helped me find my way back to my true essence, and now there's no way I can live anything less than that truth. I will always be grateful to you."

"I appreciate that," Maya reflected. "My greatest wish is for my clients to find their center in love itself—unconditional, inclusive, and compassionate. A love that doesn't judge or exclude. It simply exists as a force, an inner power, that connects us all, guiding us towards kindness, understanding and care for one another. Abundance can always be found there."

As the video call faded to black, Mirabel sat in the quiet, feeling whole in a way she'd never known before. It seemed impossible that traveling with Leila, and then the random encounter with Lawrence which led her to Maya, had opened so many doors. Yet these moments, strung together like pearls, had awakened her to a truth she'd always carried within: the endless possibility of who she could become. She knew that while this chapter with Maya was ending, a new one was just beginning.

That night, as Mirabel prepared for bed, a sense of anticipation filled her. Change was coming and she could feel it in the air, electric with possibility.

A few weeks later, Mirabel felt... different. But she decided to make sure before sharing it with Ethan.

That evening, they cuddled on the sofa, a soft blanket draped over their legs. A lamp bathed the living room in a warm glow. Outside the window, the usual San Francisco summer fog had rolled in, blanketing the city.

After sharing the details of their day, Ethan turned to Mirabel, his expression thoughtful. "Can I share something with you?"

She settled back into the couch, giving him her full attention. "Of course."

He was quiet for a moment, gathering his thoughts. "You know, watching you these past months—seeing how you've grown, how you've faced your fears... it's changed me too." He paused, his voice gentle and vulnerable. "I used to think being strong meant having all the answers. But seeing you work through things with such courage, it's taught me there's strength in being honest about our struggles."

"You're sensing that vulnerability is its own kind of strength?" she reflected, her eyes warm with understanding.

"You're," he nodded, encouraged by her presence. "And it's more than that. Watching you trust yourself, trust life—it's helped me recognize my own patterns. How I sometimes hold back because I'm afraid of making mistakes." His fingers found hers. "But now I'm learning that taking those small, steady steps forward, even when we're uncertain... that's how we build the life we dream about."

She squeezed his hand gently, hearing the deeper truth in his words.

"You know what else?" he continued, his voice growing softer. "Seeing you work with Maya, watching how you're helping your mom and Sarah now—it's shown me that transformation isn't just personal. It ripples out, touches everyone around us." He smiled. "Even me."

They leaned closer, his arm finding its way around her. "This journey," he murmured, "It's been more than I ever expected. Thank you for bringing me along with you."

Mirabel nestled against him, letting the weight of his words settle in the quiet between them. No response was needed—her presence, her understanding, was enough. In the peaceful silence that followed, she felt the perfect rightness of this moment. Her heart beginning to race, she gave his hand another gentle squeeze. "I have something amazing to share too."

He squeezed back, smiling. "What is it?"

"I love you so much, and..." She paused and pulled that morning's pregnancy test out of her pocket and handed it to him, grinning.

"Are you serious?" he gasped, eyes wide with wonder. "Is this for real?" His face broke into a radiant smile and he pulled her close and shouted with joy. "We're going to be parents? I'm going to be a dad?!"

Happy tears spilling down her cheeks. They held each other, the joy between them almost incandescent.

"How long have you known? How are you feeling?" he asked, cradling her face.

"This morning," she laughed through her tears. "I'm over the moon!"

Ethan leaned down to her stomach. "Hello, little one. We can't wait to meet you." He kissed her belly. "I love you both so much."

As they sat wrapped in bliss, Mirabel thought about their journey and the abundance they'd discovered. Now, a new chapter was beginning—one they would all write together.

A few nights after telling Ethan she was pregnant, Mirabel fell asleep. Her mind swirled with newfound insights.

In her dream...

Mirabel was in a sun-drenched kitchen, swaying gently, a toddler nestled against her chest. Ethan entered, kissing them both, his eyes radiating love. Mirabel noticed her paintings tucked in a corner ready for delivery to a local gallery.

The scene shifted to her studio, where Mirabel worked on a large canvas. Her brush strokes were confident and free bringing to life a vibrant landscape of forests and streams. At the center, a diverse community gathered.

Next, she led a dynamic team in an open office space, collaborating on innovative products to make the world better. Ideas flowed freely, and every voice was valued.

The dream shifted to evening, where golden light spilled across Mirabel and Ethan's backyard. Her mother, sister, Leila, Tanya and other friends gathered for a potluck dinner, sharing dishes made with care in their own kitchens. Though she couldn't see him clearly, Mirabel sensed her father's presence hovering at the edges of the gathering, like a familiar shadow.

As stories and laughter floated on the warm air, and plates passed from hand to hand, Mirabel watched her loved ones with a full heart, deeply grateful for the web of relationships that had shaped her life.

As the dream faded, Mirabel realized her view of life had shifted entirely. Where she once saw scarcity, she now perceived endless possibilities. Gentle self-acceptance enveloped her, nurturing a newfound appreciation for her own worth. She saw joy in her child's smile, her work's creativity, her family's warmth, and her love for Ethan.

Mirabel drifted awake, feeling peaceful down to her toes. The morning light painted patterns on her wall as understanding settled over her like a warm blanket: abundance had been here all along. It lived in everyday moments—in freely given love, in ideas that wouldn't stay quiet, in connections that grew stronger with time. She had everything she needed, and somehow, that made everything more than enough.

The fears that had once gripped her now felt like distant echoes. Her hand drifted to her belly, and she smiled. *This is no dream*, she thought. *This is my life.* As she rose to meet the day, sunlight warming her face, Mirabel felt ready for whatever beautiful surprises lay ahead.

FINAL WORD

As I write these final words, I reflect on our journey together. We began with a simple question about feeling "not enough." Through Mirabel's story and the Money Catalyst, we've discovered pathways to living fully and freely. More than that, we've learned to reject the comfortable limitations that once defined our lives, choosing instead to embrace the full spectrum of what's possible.

Life's profound lessons often come unexpectedly. When my husband received his cancer diagnosis at 56, everything shifted. It became a stark reminder that we don't get unlimited chances to live the life we're capable of living. Instead of clinging to routine, I chose to step away—to spend more time with him, to travel, to connect, to improve my own health, to live differently. What seemed like an ending became a beginning, my own catalyst forcing me to confront the gap between the life I was living and the life that was possible.

The transformation that started in Paris has touched every part of my life. I've learned that abundance isn't just appreciating life's gifts—it's letting them transform us into the people we're meant to become. I see it in my daughter's problem-solving spirit, my son's depth of insight, and my husband's unwavering love and support. My clients, who are also dear friends, came together to help shape this book in ways I never imagined possible, making it better for each of you. Each of them refused to accept the ordinary, pushing both themselves and this work toward excellence.

Most remarkably, I've learned to embrace life's shadows—challenges I once avoided now feel like essential threads in my story. I hope you've discovered this truth as well. Life isn't only about celebrating triumphs, but recognizing how each difficulty shapes us into stronger, wiser versions of ourselves. When we refuse to live small, when we reject the easy comfort of limitation, these challenges become stepping stones rather than stumbling blocks.

The journey we've shared through these pages is about choosing to live in full color rather than shades of grey. It's about refusing to accept the life that circumstance hands us and instead create the life we know, deep in our hearts that we're meant to live.

As you close this book, remember: your path is uniquely yours. Trust your inner wisdom, not the voices that whisper "settle for less." Let joy surprise you in moments big and small, and know you deserve every ounce of abundance that comes your way. In sharing your stories—struggles and triumphs alike—you weave yourself into a larger tapestry of connection. It reminds you that you are meant for more than mere existence.

You were born for abundance, joy, and connection—nothing less than the full expression of your potential. Becoming your own catalyst not only means questioning old beliefs relentlessly, it leads to something truly precious—the power to create a vibrant life without limitation. True wealth isn't measured by the numbers in your bank account, but by the richness of your experiences, the depth of your relationships, and the courage to live authentically. It's about having the audacity to recognize what truly matters and claim it as your own.

Thank you for walking this path with me, for daring to imagine more for yourself. May your journey forward be rich with discovery, filled with moments that remind you that you were meant to soar, not crawl. Know that you'll always have more than enough to share when you refuse to live beneath your potential.

With deep gratitude and belief in your unlimited possibilities,

Leisa

Claim Your Free Gifts Now!

Register at www.moneycatalystbook.com to receive meditations for clarity, a 47-page Money Catalyst Journal, and access to free workshops.

For practical and therapeutic advice about money mindset, pick up a copy of **The Mindful Millionaire**.

Ready to Take Your Financial Journey Further?

Discover Leisa's coaching and exclusive retreats blending mindfulness with financial strategies by connecting:

Email: lpeterson@wealthclinic.com

Instagram: @leisapeterson

Facebook Group: The Mindful Millionaire Community

If you enjoyed this book, please leave a review on Amazon, Barnes & Noble, Goodreads, or wherever you purchased it. Your feedback helps other readers discover this work. Thank you!

THE DEEPER JOURNEY

QUESTIONS FOR REFLECTION

Now that you've traveled with these characters through their transformations, witnessed their courage in facing difficult truths, and perhaps seen reflections of your own journey within their stories, you might find yourself with lingering thoughts, stirred emotions, or a sense that there's more to discover beneath the surface.

These questions are an invitation to go deeper—not just with the story, but with yourself. Consider reading through the book again, this time with pen in hand and heart open to what resonates most personally. Let the characters' experiences become mirrors for your own insights, struggles, and growth.

There's no rush to answer everything at once, and no "right" way to engage with these reflections. Some questions may spark immediate recognition, while others might take time to unfold. Trust your instincts about which ones call to you in each moment. The goal isn't completion—it's connection: to the story, to your own truth, and to the healing that comes when we're brave enough to look within.

Your journey through these pages was just the beginning. Now, if you're ready, let the real exploration begin.

Catalyst One

1. What does living a joyful and abundant life mean to you?

2. Which character(s) do you most identify with and why?

3. What meaningful coincidences did you notice between Mirabel and Lawrence's meeting?

4. Have similar coincidences helped move your life forward? If so, reflect on those experiences.

Catalyst Two

1. Recall a time when resources felt scarce. What fears drove your decisions during that period? How did you respond?

2. How do your friends and family approach resources differently than you? What patterns do you notice from witnessing their behavior?

3. Think about a time when you felt overwhelmed, like Mirabel, by multiple challenges. What emotions surfaced?

4. How did you cope with this process and what did you learn about yourself? What assumptions about yourself and others turned out to be untrue?

5. Think back to a key moment that shaped how you view success. What happened, and how did it change what you believed was possible for you?

6. When you consider where you came from—your family, your community, your early experiences—how has that shaped the way you pursue your goals today?

7. What's the biggest challenge you've faced in creating the life you want? What surprised you about how you handled it?

8. Mirabel realizes she needs to make some changes in her life and asks for help. Are there places in your life where you could ask others for their assistance or support?

9. What did you learn from Maya and Mirabel's first conversation?

10. Take a few minutes to breathe and center yourself. An image appears of a younger you when you first realized being abundant, joyful or free was something you wanted. Where were you, how old were you, what were you feeling at the time, why did you want to feel this way?

11. Reflect on a time when you stood up for your needs with someone close to you. How did it affect your relationship and what did you learn?

12. In what ways do your thoughts, feelings, and behaviors about 'enough-ness' influence your life and relationships? How might shifting these patterns impact your personal growth and connections with others?

13. As you reflect on A.W.A.K.E., what steps do you believe will be most helpful to support your vision of a fulfilling life?

14. In what ways do you currently show love and approval for yourself? What are some new ways you can practice greater self-love and compassion?

Catalyst Three

1. Find a comfortable position, close your eyes, and take three deep, slow breaths. Picture yourself as a young child. Connect with this younger version of yourself and gently ask: When did you feel most safe and whole? What created that feeling of safety for you? Beneath your desire for money and success, what do you most want to heal in your life?

2. Consider how Maya states that we possess an infinite power ready to be utilized. What does that mean to you?

3. Write down five to ten "I am" statements that resonate.

4. Reflect on balancing between your own needs and those of others.

5. Reflect on a significant childhood disappointment or unmet need. How might this experience be influencing your current relationships and thought patterns? Consider both obvious and subtle ways this could be shaping your present life.

6. Reflect on any recurring thoughts or beliefs about yourself, considering both empowering and limiting ones.

7. Journal about your own money "backstory" similar to what Mirabel shares about Ethan and herself.

8. Reflecting on your personal history and current life, in what ways do you recognize the influence of Scare City? How has it shaped your relationships, decisions, and self-perception? What emotions arise as you consider shifting away from these influences? What fears, if any, could challenge this shift, and how can you approach them with compassion?

9. As you envision yourself in the Abundant World, what resonates most deeply? How does it contrast with your reality, and what emotions arise as you consider this?

10. Reflect on a recent challenge. How might you approach this differently by embodying the Abundant World? What new possibilities or perspectives emerge?

11. The passage suggests creating an 'inner temple' of abundance. What would yours look and feel like?

<u>Catalyst Four</u>

1. Think about your current life circumstances—your relationships, career, and personal growth. What Acres of Diamonds might you be overlooking?

2. Reflect on a recent conflict or misunderstanding in an important relationship. How might applying the principles of open-mindedness and renewed appreciation, as demonstrated by Ethan and Mirabel, change your approach to resolving such issues? What opportunities for growth might emerge from this new perspective?

3. Reflect on a time when you felt conflicted between achieving success and staying true to your principles and values. What did this experience reveal about the nature of true fulfillment and the potential costs of compromising integrity?

4. Reflect on your earliest memories and experiences with money. How have these shaped your current beliefs about wealth, not having enough, and your relationship with finances? Consider both positive and negative associations. What fears or limiting beliefs about money might be influencing your decisions and overall sense of well-being today?

5. Consider your Limiting Beliefs about money and then ask yourself: What scares you the most about money? What problems in the past remain unresolved? Is there anyone, including yourself, you haven't forgiven around money? What do you wish you could change with money? What do you most enjoy

about money? Go through A.W.A.K.E. with any limiting beliefs you uncover.

6. Reflect on a specific moment in the story that struck a chord
   with you. Identify one past experience or recurring habit that
   you feel is hindering or supporting your goals. How has this
   experience or habit impacted your progress?

7. Maya teaches about finding benefits in difficulties. Think of
   a recent challenge you faced. How might reframing it as an
   opportunity for growth change your perspective or approach?
   When has fear of not being "good enough" led you to act in ways
   that didn't align with your values? What helped, or could help,
   you find your way back to being true to yourself?

8. Think about someone who has helped you through a difficult
   moment, like Maya did for Mirabel. What made their support
   so meaningful? What did they help you see about yourself?

9. Reflect on a situation where you felt constrained by someone
   else's expectations or rules. How could you communicate your
   need for autonomy and trust in a way that's both assertive and
   respectful?

10. Think back to a time when you had to choose between being
    smart with your money and doing something that would make
    you happy. What did you learn from that experience? How
    would you handle a similar situation today?

Catalyst Five

1. Reflect on your personal definition of freedom, considering both material and non-material aspects of life. How do your core values shape this definition, and in what ways have these values guided you through challenging situations?

2. Consider your role in your community and relationships, journal about what arises.

3. How have people in your life influenced your growth, and how have you contributed to the growth of others?

4. How can you create meaningful experiences or conversations to deepen your connections with those closest to you? Consider a shared activity, resource (like a book or workshop), or discussion that could enrich your relationships.

5. What specific qualities or actions make you feel supported? How might you cultivate more of these behaviors in your relationships?

6. If you could wave a magic wand that allows you to travel anywhere, where would you want to go and why?

7. Invite a friend or family member to share about one of their abundant experiences and take time to share your experiences with them.

8. Looking ahead, what experiences or opportunities, if any, do you feel drawn to exploring that could contribute to a greater

sense of joy and abundance?

<u>Catalyst Six</u>

1. Take a moment to connect with your inner wisdom—the compassionate, supportive, and guiding voice within you that encourages you to reach your fullest potential. Reflect on where you would like to be in one, three, and five years?

2. In your journal, reflect on how you can cultivate deeper trust with yourself, especially with financial decisions and feeling like you are wealthy, free and living your best life. In what ways can you support yourself when doubt arises?

3. What have you learned about increasing your income and savings from this chapter?

4. Does your current income level provide for a healthy financial state of well-being and if so, reflect on why that is. If not, then write about what amount you'd like to earn and why.

5. Which of Maya's income-increasing strategies most resonate with you and why? If you want to increase your income, what action can you take now?

6. Which of Maya's savings-increasing strategies most resonate with you and why? If you want to increase your savings, what action can you take now?

7. Reflect on how you've approached personal finance. Have you focused on cutting expenses, increasing income, a combination of both or neither?

8. What are you learning from this story that could be applied to your finances?

9. When it comes to building wealth, do you hold onto any beliefs relating to your current financial situation, your age, or other factors that limit how you approach the future? If so, what would you like to change and why?

Catalyst Seven

1. Reflect on a recent important decision you made. How might you have approached it differently using Maya's three-step process Prepare, Reflect and Act with trust? What new insights or outcomes might this approach have revealed?

2. Consider a current challenge or opportunity in your life. Can you apply this process to that situation?

3. Think about your long-term goals and values. What small step can you take today to move towards more joy?

4. Consider an area of your life where you've been holding onto negativity or past mistakes. How might applying forgiveness and self-compassion change your approach to this situation?

5. Are you willing to change your beliefs, thoughts, behaviors, and actions, if it means greater wealth and freedom in your life?

6. Envision a choice or decision you've been wanting to make in your own life. Consider how you can make that decision so that it creates opportunity for "more" in your life.

Catalyst Eight

1. Is there a moment that sparked realizations of abundance in your life? Why was it so impactful for you? What did it teach you about what 'having enough' really means?

2. Think about a time when you felt truly content or fulfilled. What were you doing? Who were you with? What made this moment stand out from others, and how can you create more moments like this?

3. What have you discovered about yourself and your life by reading and journaling through this book?

4. Which of the Eight Catalysts are calling to you and why would it help you to focus on them?

5. What activities or moments in your life bring you the greatest joy? How can you create more space for these experiences? What daily practice or ritual will you commit to that will help keep you anchored in abundance?

6. Write a letter to yourself about how proud you are for who you've become (and are becoming) through this experience.

7. Like Mirabel, what dreams are you ready to paint into reality?

Acknowledgements

Never in my dreams did I think this sort of book would become possible, and yet here it is. I am humbly and deeply thankful to every person who helped in its creation. Great things happen because teams of dreams are assembled to make them happen.

To my husband Tim, who worked ceaselessly with me to ensure readers would have an enjoyable experience. His endless questions and supportive thoughts helped me learn how to improve and perfect this story. Your boundless love and devotion have transformed my life into something more beautiful than I ever imagined possible.

To my incredibly inspired friend Jenny Joy and my talented writing team—Catherine Greenspan, Elizabeth Ann Atkins, and Brynn Breuner—your guidance and inspiration have made this book possible. The care, consideration, and love you showed in helping me perfect these pages is something I will always treasure deeply.

I am grateful to The Mindful Millionaire community, especially Stacey Reid, Mia Gentile, Deb Connaway, Simone Griffin, Steven Morris and Ghia Johnson, whose insights and feedback helped shape this story and ensure it resonates with diverse voices and experiences. Special thanks to my long-time clients who demonstrated that these principles truly work.

Thank you to my long-time friend Robert Spano for inspiring many of the tips Maya shares with Mirabel and parts of her story. You were my first mentor when it came to questioning popular assumptions about personal finance in the 1990's and it changed my life as a result.

To you, my readers: Thank you for reading, absorbing, and using these principles, and for sharing them with those you love. I hope this book makes your spirit soar, your wallet grow, and your soul flourish as you share what you learn with others. Thank you for reading and for never giving up on your dreams.

About the Author

Leisa Peterson is dedicated to transforming millions of lives through heightened financial consciousness. As a financial intuitive, strategic advisor, and author of The Mindful Millionaire, Leisa's journey is marked by an unwavering commitment to personal growth.

Through her unique blend of financial expertise and mindset coaching, Leisa empowers clients to master their finances with clarity and confidence. Her signature approach goes beyond numbers, instilling a strategic money mindset that fuels growth, boosts confidence, and enables people from all walks of life to make empowered, forward-focused decisions.

Central to her philosophy is the conviction that abundance is an attainable reality for all. With a three-decade tenure in finance, Leisa guides leaders, entrepreneurs, and teams as they navigate the complex intersection of money, identity, and vision, particularly during pivotal crossroads.

Recognized by Forbes as one of the pioneering "10 Women Driving Growth in Wealth Management and Investing," Leisa hosts "The Mindful Millionaire" and "Art of Abundance" podcasts. Her insights can be found on Gaia Media Network, Wall Street Journal, FastCompany, The Week, and Huffington Post. In 2023, she was awarded the "Women Who Roar" Illuminator award by SRQ Magazine, and she continues to empower clients through online workshops and transformative in-person retreats.

Leisa lives in Sedona, AZ with her husband Tim. They have successfully launched two children—one studying engineering at ASU and the other thriving in her own entrepreneurial journey—and cherish that both kids still love coming home to visit.

How to Start a Money Catalyst Discussion Group/Book Club

Creating Your Money Catalyst Discussion Group

Exploring the Eight Catalysts with others can enhance your experience and deepen your practice:

Form a group — Start or join a regular discussion group focused on the Eight Catalysts so you can:

- Gain fresh perspectives from other participants

- Receive compassionate support on your journey

- Create accountability for implementing practices

- Share experiences in a safe, loving environment

Remember: The Money Catalyst is not itself the truth, but a pathway to discovering the truth that already resides within you. Through group study and practice, you bring forth your own inner wisdom and understanding

Suggested Format

Anyone can form a group and come up with their own format and the group runs independently of WealthClinic and Leisa Peterson. I suggest that each meeting be centered on a particular catalyst/chapter that was chosen during the previous group meeting. You may wish to allow a few minutes for silent meditation or breathing practice.

Guidelines for The Money Catalyst Book Group:

To embody and reflect an attitude of mutual openness, compassion and support:

- Create a safe and compassionate environments in which to explore, share and put into practice what you are learning.

- No one should act as the teacher, or try to dominate the group.

- When someone shares, do not judge what they are sharing. Only give feedback if it is asked for.

- Everyone who comes to a meeting should have these guidelines available to them.

Quick-Start Checklist

Before your first Money Catalyst meeting:

- Decide on group size (5-12 members is often ideal)

- Choose meeting frequency (monthly is most common)

- Select your meeting location and send invitations with details

Suggested Declaration to State When Starting Each Session

"Group Confidentiality Agreement: Everything shared here stays here. Personal stories and experiences are not to be discussed outside this group without explicit permission from the speaker. This creates the safety needed for authentic sharing. By participating, you commit to this confidentiality. Do you agree?"

Discussion Starters For Each Catalyst

Keep these handy for exploring each catalyst:

"How did this catalyst resonate with your personal financial journey?"

"What resistance or barriers did you notice within yourself while reading this catalyst?"

"What specific practice from this catalyst will you implement this week?"

"How does this catalyst challenge conventional financial wisdom?"

"What new insight about your relationship with money emerged while studying this catalyst?"

"Which exercise in this chapter had the strongest impact on you?"

"How might this catalyst transform your financial decisions moving forward?"

"What connections do you see between this catalyst and the ones we've explored previously?"

Your Journey Together

Your Money Catalyst group starts with these teachings, but it will ultimately be defined by the community.

Beyond finances: Your group creates space for inner truth to emerge and perspectives to broaden

Shared growth: The real transformation happens when diverse viewpoints unite around a commitment to inner financial work

Community impact: The connections you build extend far beyond money conversations

Make it yours: While starting with these teachings, your group will be uniquely shaped by the conscious community you create together

Well wishes: May your collective journey toward financial and spiritual abundance be richly rewarding!

www.ingramcontent.com/pod-product-compliance
Lightning Source LLC
Chambersburg PA
CBHW070607120726
47909CB00007B/2479